ROARING AT THE DAWN

BRIAN JACKMAN

ROARING AT THE DAWN

JOURNEYS IN WILD AFRICA

PHOTOGRAPHS BY JONATHAN SCOTT
AND DAVID COULSON

SWAN·HILL
PRESS

For Annabelle

Copyright © 1995 by Brian Jackman

First published in the UK in 1995
by Swan Hill Press an imprint of Airlife Publishing Ltd

British Library Cataloguing in Publication Data
  A catalogue record for this book
  is available from the British Library

ISBN 1 85310 570 8

Typeset by Hewer Text Composition Services, Edinburgh.
Printed in Italy

Swan Hill Press
an imprint of Airlife Publishing Ltd
101 Longden Road, Shrewsbury SY3 9 EB

Contents

GABON

CONGO

ZAIRE

UGANDA

Lake Turkana

KENYA

L. Baringo

Samburu Nat Park

Aberdare Nat Park

Meru Nat Reserve

Kora

L. Nakuru

Maasai Mara

Mount Kenya

L. Naivasha

NAIROBI

Mt Kilimanjaro & Nat Park

Lake Victoria

L. Natron

Serengeti

Ngorongoro Conservation Area

Mt Meru

Arusha

Tsavo Nat Park

Lamu Is.

Malindi

L. Eyasi

Ngorongoro Crater

Manyara Nat Park

Arusha Nat Park

Tarangire Nat Park

Mombasa

L. Manyara

TANZANIA

DAR ES SALAAM

Zanzibar

Ruaha Nat Park

Mikumi Nat Park

L. Rukwa

Lake Banguela

L. Malawi

Selous Game Reserve

S. Luangwa Nat Park

ANGOLA

ZAMBIA

MALAWI

MOZAMBIQUE

Lusaka

Kunene River

Lake Kariba

Kariba

Mana Pools Nat Park

River Zambezi

Victoria Falls

Matusadona Nat Park

HARARE

Etosha Pan

Kasane

Etosha Nat Park

Caprivi Strip

Chobe Nat Park

Hwange

Eastern Highlands

Skeleton Coast Park

Okavango Delta

Moremi Wildlife Res

ZIMBABWE

Chief's Island

Maun

Bulawayo

NAMIBIA

Hwange Nat Park

Matobo Hills Nat Park

Swakopmund

WINDHOEK

Central Kalahari Game Reserve

Mashatu Game Reserve

Gonarezhou Nat Park

Namib Desert

Kalahari Desert

EASTERN TRANSVAAL

Kruger Nat Park

Malamala

BOTSWANA

Londolozi

Namib-Naukluft Park

GABARONE

Pretoria

JOHANNESBURG

SWAZILAND

Orange River

SOUTH AFRICA

Ladysmith

NATAL

Drakensberg Mtns

LESOTHO

Durban

THE CAPE

Wine Routes

Garden Route

East London

CAPE TOWN

Kynsna

Port Elizabeth

The Equator

Tropic of Capricorn

Atlantic Ocean

Indian Ocean

Introduction

Very carefully, before turning off the light, I looked under the bed for lurking cobras and poisonous baboon spiders. My room was on the ninth floor of the Nairobi Hilton, but my precautions did not strike me as ludicrous at the time. Nairobi was Africa, where everything bites, and this was my first time in it.

Twenty years and many safaris later it is easy to laugh at the tenderfoot who was myself. But the fact remains that fear of snakes and other crawling things deters many people who might otherwise consider going on safari. Why visit a continent where snakes and scorpions abound, where even to dip a toe into the most inviting stream is to risk catching bilharzia, and where there is always the chance, no matter how slight, of being gored, trampled or even eaten by some of the larger denizens?

For me the answer is simple. There is nowhere on earth so wild or so beautiful as the African bush, and the fact that it is also the home of many potentially dangerous animals adds a certain frisson which sharpens the senses and instils a proper sense of respect.

It is important to remember that the bush is not a zoo. The animals are truly wild and all of them — even the deceptively ponderous hippo — can run much faster than you. Yet it would be wrong to dwell too much on the hazards. Most game-viewing is conducted from the safety of lodge verandahs or Land-Rovers, and the animals have become used to tourists.

Often, when I was watching the lions of the Masai Mara Game Reserve in south-west Kenya, the big pride males would seek the shade of my vehicle out on the treeless plains and slump down beneath the open window, close enough for me to touch had I been so foolish.

Such close encounters are uncommon, however, as are the times when you may be witness to a kill. Yet the possibility is always there. To a casual eye the African savannah may appear as peaceful as an English park, but those endless vistas of golden grass conceal sudden, violent images: half-eaten zebras, bloated vultures, hyenas thrusting red muzzles into a wreck of ribs. Such sights are not for the squeamish.

Yet in the end it is not the drama or the brief moments of savagery that get to you, but the sense of space and distance. In the great emptiness of the Serengeti the land reaches out to a horizon so faintly blue and far away that it seems like the edge of the world. And the light is not like the soft watercolour skies of home. In the pure air of the Masai highlands it is diamond bright. Its peculiar clarity, falling across the open plains, makes for a wild and heady sense of freedom; and never more so than in the golden hour, that magical time towards sundown when the air begins to cool and the game is on the move again as lions stir and cheetahs emerge to hunt among the lengthening shadows.

All the best safaris begin with a map. It is at once the most invaluable and the most evocative travel document ever devised. Looking at my disintegrating map of Botswana — a precious talisman of a journey I made across the Central Kalahari Game Reserve in 1983 — it takes no great leap of the imagination to translate its arid browns and yellows into those immense southern African thirstlands: here is where we camped out under the stars in lion country, and there is where we punctured our fuel tank, and plugged it, successfully, with soap.

When I was a boy growing up in the anonymous streets of suburban Surrey, maps were the tangible evidence of the wider horizons I could not see. They were an escape route, a passport to journeys of the mind to places I had read about and longed to visit, yet which seemed as remote to me then as the dark side of the moon.

Eagerly I devoured the tales of travel and adventure my father brought home from the library. He was an avid reader of big-game hunting books, and it was not long before I, too, knew the Swahili names for all the animals: *chui* (leopard), *ndovu* (elephant), *simba* (lion). It was then, following the footsteps of old-time elephant hunters like Karamoja Bell across the burning thornscapes of those pages, that I learned to yearn for Africa.

Even now, my old school atlas (1940, most of the globe a rich colonial pink) still falls open at Africa. There it lies, that huge, dusty continent, shaped like an elephant's ear and littered with the names that echoed in my imagination like talking drums. Zambezi, Nairobi, Kilimanjaro, Okavango, Ngorongoro — they had stolen my soul away.

Now, forty years on, I know parts of the Masai country better than my own. I have travelled by camel through Samburuland, driven down the desolate shores of Namibia's Skeleton Coast and followed Livingstone through the swamps of Lake Bangweulu.

By the time I arrived, the shadows had begun to reach out across Africa. The monsoon winds no longer brought odysseys of dhows to Mombasa and Zanzibar. The ivory holocaust which was about to sweep away three-quarters of a million elephants was just beginning, and the day of the rhino was almost done. But at least I was in time to catch the twilight of the days when the going was good, out in the yellow grasslands where you can still hear the lions roaring at the dawn.

This is the Africa I would like to share with the reader. Much of its sweetness still remains, if you know where and how to find it, as those who have been will know. The following pages, culled from two decades of safari notebooks, are offered both as a celebration of wild Africa and as a guide to some of its enduring glories. I hope you enjoy your safari.

Brian Jackman
POWERSTOCK, DORSET, ENGLAND. MARCH 1995.

Chapter One
Where the Marsh Lions Roam

Fat African raindrops spattered against the Land-Rover windscreen. On the western horizon the Aberdares lay as dark as a bruise, with the summits of the Kinangop sulking in cloud. Only three weeks earlier, cattle had been dying in Kenya's worst drought for half a century. But at last the short rains had come. Now the fertile Kikuyu highlands were as green as Switzerland, and the murram roads had become rivers of red earth. '*Matope mingi*,' sighed my Kikuyu driver as we slithered on towards the Aberdare Country Club. 'Much mud.'

Curry for lunch in the club's comfortable old ex-colonial dining room. Coffee on the verandah, looking out between the Cape chestnut trees across the grassy steppes of Naro Moru towards Mount Kenya. Then up into the misty Aberdares, through dripping glades and tall, mossy trees, and the first animals: warthog, bushbuck and a herd of sullen buffalo.

No wonder professional hunters treat these wild black cattle with such respect. At first they ran; but then they whirled to face us, heads up, wet nostrils flaring, the big bulls staring from beneath the massive bosses of their horns like low-brow thugs intent on a mugging, as if they would like nothing better than to toss us over the nearest bush.

We saw no elephants, although there were plenty of fresh signs of them; but deeper in the park we surprised a magnificent forest leopard, a big, dark male padding through the rain.

At the Ark, 7,500 feet above sea level in a marshy forest glade, there was tea with cucumber sandwiches thinly sliced, a log fire in the hearth and a view through wide picture windows of the most photographed waterhole in Kenya.

The Ark, just three hours' drive from Nairobi, is a gentle introduction to wild Africa; a snug redoubt where there is no need to go jolting around in the bush looking for game. Instead, the animals come to you, lured by essential mineral salts in the waterhole's muddy banks. Darkness falls with a shrilling of frogs, and the marshy clearing with its ghostly grey herons and yellow-billed ducks is transformed into a floodlit arena, a theatre-in-the-round, where all kinds of dramas are enacted nightly.

Inside the lodge, voices are hushed. There is an air of expectancy; a sense of curtain-up. Last week an elephant gave birth in full view of the assembled visitors. Who knows what this evening may bring?

In the event it was a quiet night. A couple of buffalo, a ponderous black rhino carrying a long, thin frontal horn, and a family of giant forest hogs rootling in the mud. No elephant, no leopard, and sadly, no bongo — the rare, shy, chestnut-coloured forest antelope that once crept down from the high bamboo forests but is now almost extinct in the Aberdares.

I did not mind. There would be many more animals on the wide grass plains of the Masai Mara Game Reserve down on the Tanzanian border in south-west Kenya. Here, just forty minutes by air from Nairobi, lives the heaviest concentration of large predators and plains game in Africa.

Next day I flew through a rainstorm and landed on the dirt airstrip near Governor's Camp with zebras scudding away beneath the wing-tips. The plane slowed to a stop and I stepped down on to the wet earth, thrilled to be back in the territory of the Musiara lion pride, whose lives I had once chronicled with the photographer Jonathan Scott.

We called them the Marsh lions; one of several large prides which roam the 600-square-mile reserve. But the territorial pride males who had once been as familiar as old friends — Mkubwa with his battle-torn muzzle, Brando, the majestic Scar — were all dead. New males now ruled the Marsh, and even as I waited for the baggage to be unloaded, two huge lions I did not recognise, each with a splendid shaggy mane, trotted across the end of the airstrip, less than a hundred yards away.

The high country of the Mara usually enjoys good rains, yet here, too, the recent drought had caused great suffering. The buffalo in particular had been hard-hit. Many were just walking sacks of bones, and so weak that a lone bull — normally a formidable adversary — could be pulled down by a single male lion.

Now the drought was over and the season of rebirth and renewal had arrived, when the grass springs afresh from the parched plains and the handsome topi antelope produce their gangling ginger calves.

It did not rain continuously. The days were hot and sunny, but every afternoon stormclouds piled up over the Siria Escarpment as zebra galloped in full sunshine over the greening plains, their striped coats standing out in brilliant contrast against the deepening indigo sky.

The drumming rain caused the termite mounds to erupt. Everywhere, silver fountains of winged ants rose from the earth, attracting clouds of migrating storks which fell out of the sky to gorge themselves on this fleeting seasonal feast.

The skies in this high country are never empty. As the lions are to the grasslands, so the eagles are to the currents and thermals that swirl in the upper airs above them. Here live the tawny eagle and the black-chested harrier eagle, the handsome bateleur, rocking and tilting on outstretched wings, and the great martial eagle, the lord of the steppe, with his ermine chest and executioner's hood. Augur buzzards flaunt their bright chestnut tails. Exquisite little black-shouldered kites hover with the ease of kestrels.

And always there are the vultures, Africa's dark angels of death, spiralling over the grasslands in search of carrion.

For many years, setting out at first light to look for the Marsh lions, I had watched with envy as the two giant multi-coloured hot-air balloons rose like twin suns from behind the riverine woodlands of Little Governor's Camp, taking their passengers high into the eagles' kingdom on a ninety-minute joyride over the plains with a champagne breakfast at the end.

It had always seemed so sybaritic and unnecessary; a touch of the fairground, an exercise in gimmickry far removed from the simple, uncluttered existence that life in the bush ought to be. It was also very expensive. Yet I longed to see the mosaic of grasslands, thickets and game trails as they must appear to the high-wheeling vultures. And in the end I gave in, and was not disappointed.

Came the moment of truth. The triple gas-burners thundered in the dawn. The long flames lanced upwards. The 100 foot-high canopy swelled under the pressure of eight tons of hot air — and suddenly we were floating free.

Soon we were at treetop height, startling a fish eagle, which almost fell off its perch, and close enough for John Coleman, our pilot, to lean out and pluck a sprig of leaves from the crown of a tall *Abyssinica* tree. 'For you, madam,' he said gallantly, offering it to one of my fellow passengers. 'A Masai rose.'

There was no time for nerves. There were too many other sensations to absorb, and none so blissful as the moment when Coleman switched off the burners and we drifted in a profound silence broken only by the barking cry of a bateleur and the sounds of the bush floating up to us from 1,000 feet below.

Ballooning over Africa, I decided, is like going to heaven in a picnic hamper. Leaning comfortably on the wicker rim, I could see the coils of the Mara River glittering among its luxuriant woodlands; the blue walls of the Siria Escarpment and the great plains reaching down into the Serengeti.

Even without binoculars it was possible to pick out the distinctive shapes of animals: a lone topi standing motionless on an anthill; a group of giraffe throwing long shadows across the grass in front of Kichwa Tembo Lodge; and, most thrilling of all, a sudden stampede of zebra immediately beneath us, where two lionesses were stalking through an ungrazed meadow of red oat grass.

Eavesdropping on the big cats in such an unusual way reminded me that it was lions which had first lured me to the Mara nearly two decades ago. I heard my first wild lion here, early on a cold, bright morning. The dew still clung to the tall stems of red oat grass, and the lion was standing on a termite mound perhaps a quarter of a mile away.

Being new to Africa, I was surprised at the manner in which he roared, not gaping open-mouthed like the old MGM movie lion, but expelling the sound from deep down in his chest through half-closed jaws; with every grunt I could see his breath condensing in distinct puffs of warm air. Now, twenty years on, I am still drawn back to the Mara by the song of the lion, and its magic never palls.

It was still dark when we left Kichwa Tembo Camp. Jonathan Scott gunned the engine of his Toyota Land-Cruiser and we set off along the foot of the Siria Escarpment. Lions were roaring in the distance, as they always do before the dawn comes up over Aitong Hill. The air was as sharp as a Masai *simi* and I shivered under my sweater.

Jonathan and I were used to these early morning starts. Since the days when he had followed the lives of the Marsh lions, I had returned every year and our days always began like this. The reason was simple. Dawn is the prime time to watch predators hunting; and if, like Jonathan, you want to photograph them, you must be out on the plains before sunrise.

Our headlights picked out the ghostly shapes of zebra moving through the thornbushes at the side of the road. A shoal of green eyes became a herd of impala held fast in the beam. We switched off the lights and they bounded away into the night.

Dawn comes up fast in the Mara. Already a thin, grey light had begun to seep over the eastern horizon as we crossed the Mara River. Now, as we turned off and headed into the reserve proper, the sun rose like a huge, distended bubble, catching a long line of wildebeest in perfect silhouette as they cantered along the horizon. Another long African day was unfolding.

The low sun flooded the plains with golden light, casting long shadows across the glistening grass. Jonathan found the spot where tyre tracks from his previous journeys ran out towards a distant ridge. Even above the whine of the engine I could hear hyenas whooping and soon we saw them, loping past us in the long grass, jaws agape in a hideous grin as if in anticipation of the feast they knew lay not far off.

Lions had pulled down a wildebeest in the night. The hyenas had heard its stricken cries, followed by the tumultuous crescendo of roaring and grunting as the rest of the pride piled in. Now the scavengers were hurrying for their share, and the kill had become a battleground; but we did not linger. Instead we drove on to the ridge. There, we knew, lived a leopard and her three small cubs.

Like all leopards the mother was ill at ease on the open plains. Without rocks or trees she was vulnerable to the unwelcome attentions of lions, which were much bigger than her, or hyenas, which were more numerous.

But the ridge was ideal. It extended for more than a mile, flanked by dark groves of wild olive trees, thorny thickets and tumbled grey boulders, like elephants turned to stone, providing a million places where a leopard and her young might hide. This was the heart of her home range, a linear sanctuary also visited from time to time by the big male leopard which had sired her cubs.

Jonathan switched off the engine and we waited, scanning the ridge through binoculars. I could see the cave in which the cubs had been born, but hyraxes were sunning themselves on the ledge above; small, grey animals that looked like guinea pigs but which by some strange quirk of evolution were more closely related to the elephant. The rocks were thickly whitewashed with their crystallised urine — a monument to the incontinence of an entire species — but their peaceful presence was a sure sign that the leopard was not at home.

Ten minutes passed; ten minutes in which I willed the leopard to appear. In my mind's eye I saw her stealthy shape lurking in every shadow. Then Jonathan raised his glasses again. 'Look,' he whispered. His keen eyes had spotted a sudden movement. Something was drifting soundlessly through the grass. It was the leopard.

To my amazement she seemed quite unperturbed by the presence of our vehicle. Normally the leopard is the most elusive of cats; shy, solitary, swift to hide; a shadow in a spotted coat. The leopard is a night walker, a denizen of the dark and secret thickets, using the strategy of surprise to grab its victims, and slipping away at the first hint of an approaching vehicle.

But not this one. Tail held high in an elegant curve, she strolled nonchalantly past, only yards from where we sat entranced.

She moved with a sinuous grace. In the morning light the rosettes on her lustrous coat bloomed soft as soot, as did the necklace of black spots which adorned the white fur of her throat. We watched her stalk a hare in the long grass. She pounced with all four feet bunched beneath her like a serval cat, but missed. For a moment she stood there, tail twitching in annoyance, sniffing the air and looking back over her shoulder to fix us with eyes as pale as stones. Then she dismissed us and was gone among the rocks and thickets of the ridge.

'Even before I first set foot in Africa the leopard was the animal I wanted to see most,' said Jonathan when she had gone. His passion for leopards goes back to childhood: he grew up in England on a farm in Berkshire, where the annual treat was a visit to London Zoo. 'I can still remember standing spellbound in front of a barren enclosure in which a huge male leopard padded up and down,' he recalled. 'Occasionally it would pause and look at me through the bars before setting off again on its endless journey. That stare has haunted me ever since.'

He saw his first wild leopard in Tanzania's Serengeti National Park in 1975, while travelling overland from England to Botswana. Having studied for a zoology degree at Queen's University, Belfast, he was desperate to live and work in the African bush; but it was his artistic talent rather than academic endeavour which enabled him to fulfil his dream. After two years in Botswana he returned to Kenya to draw and photograph the teeming plains game of the Masai Mara.

Since then he has become one of East Africa's finest wildlife photographers, as well as a successful author with books on leopards, wild dogs and the Serengeti wildebeest migration to his credit. But when I first met him he was driving safari clients around the Mara for Jock Anderson, one of Kenya's most experienced professional guides.

It was in the late 1970s. I had come to the Mara on an assignment for *The Sunday Times*. Jock Anderson, whom I had met on an earlier visit, had invited Jonathan to show me the reserve. During our game drives he began to tell me about the pride of lions which lived and hunted around Musiara Marsh, near Governor's Camp.

Sitting around the campfire one evening, he showed me his photographs and also the diary in which he entered brief details of everything he had seen on each game drive. Time and time again the words 'Marsh lions,' leaped from the pages.

The name intrigued me. It had a resonance and an element of the unusual. People did not usually associate lions with marshes, and I began to see Jonathan's favourite pride as he saw them, not as an anonymous group of animals but as individuals, each one recognisable, with its own dramatic saga of hunting, mating and fighting to be told.

By now I was completely hooked on Africa and desperately wanted to write a book about it. Jonathan was eager to win recognition and a wider audience for his superb photographs. So the idea of *The Marsh Lions* was born; a collaboration which continued over the next four years as we followed the fortunes of the Musiara pride and chronicled their story as truly as we could.

Of course, the Musiara lions were not the only pride in the reserve, which has a population of around 500, including nomads from the Serengeti. Across the river from Governor's Camp is the territory of the Kichwa Tembo pride. Downstream, on opposite sides of the river, live the Seronera lions and the Paradise Plain pride. To the north, just outside the reserve, roam the Gorge pride and the Mara Buffalo pride; away to the south-east, other large prides hunt along the Talek River and around Keekorok Lodge and Ol Kiombo.

Those days spent among the Marsh lions were among the happiest of my life. Tourism in the Mara was still in its infancy. The grasslands were not yet criss-crossed with tyre tracks or overrun with visitors, and we could be alone with the pride all day long from dawn to dusk.

It was an extraordinary privilege to enter their world and observe their complex social behaviour at such close quarters. Sometimes, as we followed the pride males out on to *Mwiti Mbili* — Two Trees Plain — they would walk towards us, tongues lolling in the heat, to slump in the shade of our vehicle. There they would sprawl, resting their huge heads on their paws and treating us with stunning indifference.

The latent power concealed under their smooth, tawny coats was awesome. From time to time, Scar would look up and open his jaws in a cavernous yawn, revealing yellow canines the size of my thumbs, and I would remember the words of Myles Turner, the legendary warden of the

Serengeti: 'There is nothing in the world as pitiless as the baleful stare of a lion.'

Scar was the epitome of a male lion in his prime. From his threadbare muzzle to his black tail-tuft he was nearly ten feet long. His mane was so thick that it almost hid his ears, a glossy rug of tobacco-coloured hair, shot through with auburn glints. He was everything a pride male should be: deep-chested, powerful, with an aura about him, a way of walking with a magisterial, almost insolent swagger that reflected his fearless self-confidence.

Looking at him and Mkubwa, his pride companion, I would try to imagine what it must feel like to be a lion. Like me, Scar would have heard the wind in the grass and the mournful descant of wood doves in the noontide luggas. Were we not warmed by the same sun? There were many sensations we must have shared; but it was impossible to know what went on behind those implacable yellow eyes.

Out on the plains the air quivered and scintillated along the stony ridges. Nothing moved. Everywhere, animals rested, seeking the shade of croton thickets or scattered acacias. Warthogs withdrew into their burrows. Buffalo lay in their wallows. Elephants moved deeper into the riverine forest, cooling themselves with flapping ears. And still the lions slept on, conserving their energy; they would move only when compelled to do so by the imperatives of hunger, or sex, or the need to assert their territorial authority.

Towards sunset the cooling air would rouse them. They would sit up to see the game on the move again, the grassy horizons spiked by the horns of topi and Thomson's gazelles. Then they would haul themselves to their feet and sniff the breeze, listening with eyes half-closed as if in concentration, catching the distant sounds of zebras and wildebeest down in the Marsh. Soon their lionesses would be hunting and they would head off at a leisurely pace towards Musiara, two dark, shaggy shapes in a lion-coloured landscape of swaying grassheads and lengthening shadows.

Sometimes, too, during the wildebeest migration, we would follow the Marsh lionesses as they prepared an ambush. There were five of them altogether — the Talek Twins and the Three Sisters — five tawny cats fanning out through the long grass, bellies down, heads low, ears laid back. Then would come the sudden rush; the wild stampede of panicking wildebeest running for their lives. All except one, clasped by a lioness in a terminal embrace as she applied the classic, choking bite to the throat, and the dust drifted away to reveal the rest of the pride closing in for the kill.

The great migration transforms the Mara. It is the high point of the year, marking an end to the cool, overcast weather of July and bringing a return of hot, bright days until the onset of the November rains. No two migrations are ever quite the same, but the zebras are invariably the first to arrive, a restless vanguard, 250,000 strong, chomping down the coarse, waist-high red oat grass to open up the plains for the more selective grazers in their wake.

The wildebeest mass on the banks of the Mara River like an army laying siege, sending clouds of dust boiling up into the blue. The crossings are spectacular beyond belief, but tinged with tragedy. Over they come in a grunting, desperate avalanche, heads tossing, eyes rolling as they swim shoulder to shoulder for the opposite bank. Many do not make it. Every year, thousands are crushed or drowned or pulled under by the huge Mara crocodiles. In the aftermath of a major crossing the air is heavy with the stench of death.

For the predators, the migration heralds a season of plenty. Wherever you look the plains are black with grazing herds, and the lions grow fat. Every morning a vortex of descending vultures pinpoints the scene of a fresh kill. Every day the Marsh pride lies in wait among the reeds or along the lugga known as *Bila Shaka* — Without Fail — because you can always find lions there. For the lions of Kichwa Tembo and Paradise Plain, and even for the shiftless young nomads who have yet to win a pride and a territory, the killing is easy.

But when September comes, the wildebeest grow restless. Soon the plodding columns are heading south once again, filing away into the northern woodlands of the Serengeti, and then on through the Seronera Valley to gather on the short-grass plains around Naabi Hill and the Gol Kopjes, where they give birth in February.

So it continues, as it has done since the Pleistocene, an ancient story with no beginning and no end — only the golden sunsets and blood-red dawns, the wind in the grass and the endless wanderings of the wild herds as they follow the showers across this enormous land.

The sense of space is intoxicating; the light, the distance, the feeling that you could drive forever through this lovely country and never come to the end of it, or have enough of it. Above all it is grassland country, and the joy of driving through it is like being at sea, the seedheads hissing and waving around you, rolling away in long, billowing ridges to a horizon so faintly blue and far away that it seems like the edge of the world.

Once all this land belonged to the Masai, nomadic pastoralists with red cloaks and shining spears, who still call vultures 'the birds of the warriors', recalling the days when blood feuds and cattle raids left their toll on the plains and the winged scavengers would come to peck out the soft eyes of the dead.

Today the Masai still graze their humpbacked cattle on the surrounding rangelands, sharing the grass with the wandering game. But progress has inevitably blunted the old, clean sense of pristine wilderness. To the east, much of the Loita Plains country has gone under the plough and been turned into wheatfields. In the Mara Reserve itself, the grasslands are scarred by a maze of tyre tracks — the unsightly legacy of the days when there was no restriction as to where anyone with a four-wheel-drive vehicle might go. And so popular has the Mara become as a tourist destination that it is hard to find cheetahs or lions on a kill without a circle of watching vehicles like vultures on a carcase.

With each passing year the problems become more acute. Kenya needs tourist dollars and so does the Mara. Without the money tourism brings, the land would surely be claimed for agriculture to feed the country's fast-growing population — so making the animals pay their way is the best chance of ensuring their survival.

But there comes a point — and many conservationists who care about the Mara believe it has been reached — when the reserve can absorb no more visitors without becoming degraded, and when the wilderness experience is at risk of being devalued by sheer weight of numbers. In Africa, such decisions are tough indeed; but Kenya has an honourable reputation in the field of conservation, despite the ravages of poaching, and the Mara is still deservedly the most visited big-game stronghold in Africa.

Kenya is not my country. My roots are in England, where I was born and where I still choose to live. But there is hardly a day when I do not miss the Mara with an unbearable longing.

At such times I miss the clear morning air, the way the light falls through the lacy canopy of the acacias, and the warm smell of the sun on the grass. I miss the cheerful sound of Swahili voices around camp, the distant squealing of zebra stallions and the calls of boubou shrikes, doves and fish eagles; and I wish I was there, knowing that even now, everything is in its place; the leopards resting on their rocky ridges, the cheetahs on the plains and the lions roaring across Musiara Marsh.

The Kenyas know what the lions are saying. '*Hii nchi ya nani? Hii nchi ya nani? Yango . . . yango . . . yango.*' Whose land is this? Whose land is this? It is mine . . . mine . . . mine.

Chapter Two
To Catch a Zebra

It was the Turkana tracker who saw him first: a solitary stallion about a mile away on the open plains of Kenya's remote Northern Province. At once Don Hunt slammed the open Toyota catching truck into gear and we lurched through the cool desert dawn towards the distant grey speck which Nyangau, the eagle-eyed Turkana tracker, assured us was the Grevy's zebra whose spoor he had found the day before.

In 1977 Don Hunt was probably the best animal-catcher in Africa, and he badly wanted that zebra. If we failed, he knew its fate was sealed. Either it would be shot by poachers and its skin nailed to the floor of a rich man's penthouse. Or, driven from the open country which was its natural habitat, it would head for the bush where the lions waited.

Grevy's zebra is the world's most beautiful wild horse, and in the 1970s it seemed to be heading for extinction. Big bat ears, a mane as proud as a centurion's plumes and an elegant coat of slimline stripes immediately set it apart from its more numerous cousin, the common or Burchell's zebra. Somehow the Grevy seems altogether more exclusive. Those close-grained stripes that flicker like an op-art painting looked so much smarter when turned into a fancy handbag. In Nairobi at that time, such bags were fetching £70. You could buy an executive telephone-directory cover in hand-stitched Grevy for £40, or a Grevy-skin coat for £350. And when the World Wildlife Fund's Kenya representative wandered into a Nairobi warehouse he was offered 250 Grevy skins on the spot.

Once Grevy's zebra ranged all over what used to be known as the NFD — the Northern Frontier District. From the shores of Lake Turkana to the Tana River and on up into Somalia and Ethiopia, they ran in herds hundreds strong. In Kenya alone their numbers were put at more than 15,000. But that was in the 1960s, before large-scale poaching emptied the plains. A decade later they had vanished forever from Somalia and Ethiopia, and in Kenya, their main stronghold, numbers had fallen to no more than a thousand.

One of the first to realise that all was not well in the NFD was Don Hunt, a genial, beefy, sun-bleached American who at that time was running the Mount Kenya Game Ranch in partnership with William Holden, the Hollywood movie star. Hunt, then in his mid-forties, had thrown up a prosperous TV career in Detroit and come to live in Kenya. He had started as a hunter but soon became sickened by the blood-letting and turned trapper instead.

It was while catching animals for the Kenya government and shipping them as gifts to Ghana and Nigeria that he became aware of the Grevy's plight. 'Every time you went back,' he said, 'you couldn't help noticing there were fewer zebra around.'

Then, in 1975, Major Ian Grimwood, at that time a consultant for the International Union for the Conservation of Nature, produced a shock report on the status of the Grevy's zebra. His figures showed that Kenya's population had crashed from 15,000 to 1,500. There could only be one cause: poaching.

Clearly, something had to be done fast if the Grevy was to survive. 'So we got together with the national park wardens,' said Don Hunt, 'and went to see the government.' The result was full backing for Operation Zebra — a plan whereby Hunt was given permission to catch 140 Grevy's and move them from the NFD to the comparative safety of the game parks. Thirty or forty were to go to the Samburu Game Reserve and the remaining hundred would take their chance down in Tsavo West, the vast national park on the Tanzanian border, where they would be under the watchful eye of Head Warden Ted Goss and his helicopter-borne anti-poaching patrols.

It was a controversial scheme and Hunt himself was a controversial figure, involved in a business which raised the hackles of many conservationists. But as he said, 'Make no mistake. The Grevy is doomed outside the parks. If the poachers don't get them, the lions will. In two years they'll all be gone.'

Hunt reckoned that at least 8,000 Grevys had been poached in the last three years, sending the price of skins soaring from $150 to $2,000. 'That kind of money has pushed them into the ivory league,' he said. 'Just think about it. If there are 1,000 Grevys left, that represents $2 million still running around out there.'

The worst poachers were the well-organised gangs of Somali bandits known as the *shifta*, who were heavily armed and dangerous. When the *shifta* embarked on a raid they hired local people as porters, trackers and skinners. The gang bosses kept the perks: ivory, rhino horns and Grevy skins, while the local hired hands, who were paid only in meat or in skins and trophies from other animals, took the rest. The result was that entire areas of northern Kenya were being cleared of everything that moved, from elephants to dik-diks.

For Don Hunt the year of the zebra had begun in January 1977. When I joined him in May the operation had already cost him $28,000. Or, as he put it, 'nearly $1,000 for every zebra I've saved'.

To catch a zebra is a dangerous game. By day there was always the risk of being shot at by the *shifta*. At night, lions roamed around Hunt's camp, lured by the smell of the captive zebras shut up in their thorny *boma*.

But the biggest dangers were the plains themselves, riddled with pig-holes and unseen luggas — dried-up watercourses that loomed under your wheels as you careered through the bush at 60 mph. It was precisely such a hazard which had hospitalised two of Hunt's catching team with broken limbs the week before I arrived.

Now here I was in the same Toyota, bearing down on that lone dawn stallion. When we were still 400 yards away he broke into a canter. We increased our speed and he began to gallop. 'He's making for the bush,' yelled Hunt, and we slewed round in a choking swirl of dust to try and head him off.

Suddenly all sense of danger was forgotten in the thrill of the chase. In the excitement we missed by inches an ant-bear hole that would have buried us all. We smashed through thornbushes, pulverising them into a million fragments that flew overhead in a spattering slipstream. Clods of red earth kicked up by the zebra's hooves smashed against the windscreen.

Time and again we would close to within yards of our quarry as Ngatia, the Kikuyu catcher, stood braced inside the rubber tyre which protected his ribs, swinging the noose of the lasso on its long bamboo pole until it dangled tantalisingly close to the tossing head. But like a rugby three-quarter the zebra would jink and swerve at the last moment, leaving us floundering in a four-wheel drift.

Once more we drew alongside, and this time Ngatia made no mistake. The noose dropped over the zebra's head, the line ran out and the Toyota skidded to a stop with the stallion plunging on the end of the line like a fighting marlin.

The drill had been perfected to a fine art. The chase was always relatively short; otherwise the animal would die from exhaustion and shock. As soon as it was caught the support truck would arrive with extra hands. The idea was to grab the zebra by its ears and tail, avoiding teeth and hooves, rope its legs together, tranquillise it, patch up any wounds with antibiotics and then haul it into a crate.

'Dammit,' said Don Hunt admiringly, 'that was the smartest zebra I've ever caught in my life.' Later he admitted he would not have pursued it for so long but for the suppurating scar on its rump where it had been clawed by a lion. 'That wound was so bad he would probably have died anyway, so I took a chance.'

We caught no more zebra that day; but the following morning we tried a fresh locality, setting out an hour before dawn to be on the catching grounds while the day was still cool.

Normally the north of Kenya is an arid wilderness of sunbleached scrub and withered thorns; but the long rains had been unusually heavy and the plains were as green as an Irish meadow. The earth blossomed overnight, and we marvelled at the sight of Samburu warriors wrapped in blood-red cloaks, striding with their cattle through drifts of white storm lilies.

Beyond the slab-sided mountain of Ololokwe, strange shark-fin peaks recede into the distance, giving this enigmatic landscape the surreal perspective of a Salvador Dali painting. Here we came across the totally unexpected sight of a band of fifty Grevys. Only five years earlier, herds of one hundred were not uncommon. But constant harassment had fragmented their numbers.

Eagerly we gave chase as the sun came up over the immense horizon. Larks rose singing into the sky, and on either side of us, oryx and elands stampeded away through the flat-topped thorn trees.

Slowly we began to close the distance between ourselves and the zebra and, as I watched their dazzling black and white bodies wheeling and turning as one, kicking up a haze of dust that hung like gold in the day's first glow, it dawned on me that I was witnessing a momentous occasion. Here was a spectacle that might never be seen again: a herd of wild Grevy's zebras running as free as the wind on the plains which had been their home since the time before man was born.

Fortunately, I was wrong. When the plight of Africa's biggest zebra species became more widely known, it was given greater protection and the trade in skins subsided. Today, though it is still endangered and almost entirely confined to the arid plains and thornbush country of northern Kenya, the Grevy's numbers appear to have stabilised in the low thousands, keeping alive the glorious vision I had seen with Don Hunt on the plains beyond Ololokwe.

Northern Kenya is a harsh and unforgiving land, yet its beauty is undeniable, its wildness unsurpassed. Here, as soon as you leave the beaten track, following the elephant paths that weave their way through the orchard-like commiphora thickets, you can feel the years fall away and imagine yourself back in the Africa of a century ago, when there were no vehicles to ease your passage through the bush.

This was the age that Julian McKeand had managed to recapture, if only for a week or so at a time, by organising camel safaris into Samuru country from his home at Lewa Downs, in the shadow of Mount Kenya.

McKeand is a former game warden who at one time worked with the legendary George Adamson and later became a professional hunter at the prestigious Mount Kenya Safari Club. In the mid-1970s, after trophy hunting was banned by President Jomo Kenyatta in a vain attempt to control elephant poaching, McKeand hit on the idea of offering camel safaris to the growing numbers of tourists who were now flocking to Kenya.

Riding a camel has one great advantage over riding on horseback: no previous experience is necessary. The camels are led by a man with a rope and never move faster than walking pace, scuffing along with an effortless soft-shoe shuffle. All you have to do is to clamber aboard, sink into the padded leather saddle and cling on to the brass pommel as the animal lurches to its feet with an alarming fore-and-aft heave.

Everything, you discover, is as authentic as McKeand can make it, from the wooden camel bells clunking around the animals' necks to the ex-British Army saddles — every one a collector's item — made by Makhanbal & Sons of Bikaner, India, in the last days of the Raj.

We made a colourful caravanserai as we marched out into the chill brightness of a Kenyan desert dawn. First the six riding camels; then twenty baggage animals laden with bed rolls, cooking pots and all the paraphernalia needed for a week's camping in the African bush.

At the head of the column strode McKeand himself, and at his side sauntered the indefatigable Moloi, his gun-bearer from his hunting days, a red *shuka* wrapped around his bony haunches.

Then followed McKeand's splendid team of trackers, cooks and camel syces, most of them red-robed Laikipiak Masai, armed to the teeth with spears and elephant guns, albeit primarily for show.

As for ourselves, we were the *wageni*, the strangers, twelve innocents from Europe and the United States, who had chosen to throw off the shackles of urban living for a week's bush-bashing across northern Kenya. For the next few days we would be completely cut off from civilisation. There would be no TV or newspapers, no indoor plumbing or noise of passing traffic. Once we left base camp at Lewa Downs we would not see even so much as a tyre track. At night, protected by nothing but a flimsy mosquito net, we would sleep under the stars and listen to the lions. By day we would walk or ride in the deep silence of the hills with only the passing of a high-flying jet — a thin white trail chalked across the cloudless desert sky — to remind us of the world outside.

Every day would begin in the same way: the cold dawn coming alive to a chorus of doves; the sun's red glow igniting the rim of the still-sleeping hills — a reverie broken by the bellowing complaints of camels being harnessed: an appalling, throat-clearing noise, like someone gargling with gravel at the bottom of a well.

Bowls of hot water for washing and shaving steamed in the sharp air. Then came tea or coffee to ward off the early morning chill, followed by fresh pawpaw and eggs and bacon. Then we would break camp and mount up. It was better to travel in these first hours of the day. By midday it would be too hot to walk.

Under those huge African skies, in that wild, awesome country, I felt absurdly happy. The Masai were happy, too. Their step was light and they sang as they led the camels down the criss-cross game trails between the thorny thickets. They sang about the blue hills above us, where greater kudu roamed the stony paths. They sang about the beauty of their cows, which they valued above everything else in the world. In high, clear voices, they made up the songs as they marched along, and each impromptu solo cadenza was answered by a stirring, one-two chant of *hunhh-hunhh*, that made the hair stand up on the back of my neck.

As for the camels, they varied in colour from dusky brown to a pale, creamy suede. At first I thought them ugly and ill-tempered brutes, but in time I grew to love their lugubrious faces, their curious dignity and tireless plodding gait. How well they were named ships of the desert. Seated aloft, swaying through the amber light of early morning, we were *wageni* no longer, but lords of the desert.

Ahead lay a landscape of yawning distance thronged with gaunt hills that rose like tombstones from grey tides of bush. The air was spiced with the smell of African sage. The sun glittered among the thorns, on green bayonets of sansevieria and on the tortured blue-grey branches of the commiphora bushes whose resin produces the biblical myrrh. We marched to the mocking cries of red-billed hornbills, watched elands cantering away through the acacias, and at one point along the trail cut the fresh tracks of a big male lion imprinted in the brick-red dust.

By midday we had set up our first camp in a shady acacia grove on the banks of a sand lugga. There were Tusker beers kept cool in canvas water buckets, followed by a lunch of cold chicken and salad, and a welcome siesta.

After tea at around four o'clock, McKeand led us on an early evening stroll into a beautiful gorge of strangler fig trees and yellow-barked acacias. Baboons barked a warning at our approach, and the echo of their voices bounced from cliff to cliff, startling three male kudu with wonderful corkscrew horns. The kudu ran swiftly up a steep slope, their hooves sending a shower of stones spinning and clattering into the dry stream-bed at the foot of the gorge. Then they vanished into the hills as silently as smoke.

Back at camp, hot showers were swiftly brought in canvas buckets, and hauled up by ropes slung over a handy branch so that the water could pour down through a sprinkler rose on to the bather beneath.

Shadows lengthened. Dusk came swiftly. Already one of McKeand's pyromaniac Masai warriors had put the torch to a fire of homeric proportions, built of whole tree trunks washed down the lugga on the last flash flood, and we sat in a circle, the sparks flying upwards, while Joffrey, the young Meru cook, prepared supper.

Joffrey was a campfire wizard whose asbestos fingers seemed impervious to pain as he casually picked up burning pot lids. From beds of hot ashes he coaxed wondrous cheese soufflés and baked delicious apple pies in old ammunition boxes. 'It's a pity he can only cook on a wood fire,' McKeand said. 'He'd make a fortune in London.'

That night Joffrey fed us on steaks and fresh avocados, and later, when a hunter's moon sailed up over the trees, the talk turned to the old days, when Julian had accompanied George Adamson and Elsa, the *Born Free* lioness, on a safari to Lake Turkana.

I remembered the last time I had accompanied one of McKeand's camel safaris, following the Seya Lugga towards the Matthews Mountains with Denis Zaphiro. Like Julian, Denis was a veteran ex-hunter and game warden whose safari clients had ranged from Hemingway to Prince Charles; and I had listened spellbound as the pair of them yarned under the stars, knowing that what I was hearing were the last authentic echoes of a Kenya that has since all but vanished.

They talked of the elephant they had shot, the buffalo and rhinos that had almost ended their lives, the camps they had known, and the boundless freedom of the bush. 'You know,' said Denis, gazing into the fire with a faraway look, 'there is never a day when I do not thank God I knew this country in the old days.'

Later, when everyone had turned in, I lay on my trestle bed looking up at the stars. Although I was protected by a mosquito net the darkness made it invisible, giving the uncomfortable illusion that I was lying exposed and vulnerable to any passing predator.

Suddenly a lion began to roar, causing the camels hobbled in the lugga to shift and grumble apprehensively. In the silence that followed I could hear my heart beating. Then the lion roared again, much closer this time, its harsh voice tailing off in a throaty series of rasping grunts that seemed to shake the air. I felt for the first time the fear of the preyed-upon.

I thought, this is how it must be for the zebras whose squeals of alarm now rang out in the black and silver night. I stared into the shadows, trying to pick up the slightest movement, straining my ears for the stealthy pad of velvet paws. But the lion did not roar again, and in the end I pulled the blanket over my head and slept soundly until dawn.

After a while, the days settled into a comfortable pattern. All sense of time forgotten, we rose with the sun, walked while it was still cool, sought the shade at noon and slept early. This was life as it ought to be, stripped of all trivia and greed; sweet and clean, but also tinged with sadness for a wilderness which I knew even then could not last for ever. McKeand knew it, too. 'In the old days,' he said, 'you could never have walked through this country without a rhino steaming out of the bush and scattering the camels.'

Now the day of the rhino is almost done. It is still a good world to walk in. Yet as I followed McKeand across that magnificent emptiness to the clank of camel bells and the song of the Masai whose words I did not understand, it seemed to me that I was listening to a requiem for a vanishing Africa, soon to be a memory, like the rhinos which once roamed this land and are dust.

Julian McKeand's account of his safari to Lake Turkana with George Adamson and Elsa had whetted my appetite. It was a place I had wanted to visit ever since I had read John Hillaby's marvellous book, *Journey to the Jade Sea*. Hillaby had done it the hard way, travelling by camel from Wamba, just south of the Matthews range. That was in the early 1960s, before tourism had penetrated as far as this remote corner of East Africa. Nowadays it is possible to fly to the lake in comfort, or drive by Land-Rover. Even so, driving is no soft option. The seven-hour trip from Maralal to Turkana is the overland equivalent of going round Cape Horn.

Top: Mother cheetah and her cub in Kenya's Masai Mara reserve. *(Brian Jackman)*

Bottom: The author (left) with Jonathan Scott, taken while following 'The Marsh Lions' in 1980. *(Brian Jackman)*

Top: The Marsh Lions: the pride which Jonathan Scott and the author observed for five years in the Masai Mara. *(Jonathan Scott)*

Bottom: Mkubwa, Brando and Scar – the three resident males of the Marsh Lion pride resting near Governor's Camp. *(Jonathan Scott)*

Top: Lioness stalking in long grass. The males provide security for the pride, but the females are the most efficient hunters. *(Jonathan Scott)*

Bottom: Tension in the pride: a male lion threatens a ten-week-old cub on the carcass of an elephant. *(Jonathan Scott)*

Top: The Masai Mara belongs to the Masai – a warrior tribe of pastoralists whose cattle share the high plains with the wild herds. *(Jonathan Scott)*

Bottom: The greatest wildlife spectacle on earth: the Serengeti wildebeest migrating across the Mara River. *(Jonathan Scott)*

Maralal, the administrative centre of the Samburu country, is a far cry from the hot, dry lowlands. It is surrounded by cedar forests and high, rolling downs which, after rain, could almost be somewhere in Surrey. But all too soon the green hills are left behind. Ahead lie the dusty El Barta Plains, deserted except for small groups of Beisa oryx and Grevy's zebra; and beyond, quivering in the desert's brassy glare, a mirage of splintered mountains.

At Baragoi, a soulless township of tin-roofed *dukas*, someone stole our petrol cap. The road — a generous term to describe the bone-shaking track — was atrocious. By the time we reached the South Horr Gorge it had given out altogether and we were lurching from boulder to boulder over what appeared to be a dry stream-bed.

By now the heat was at furnace pitch, the landscape stunned and supine. Even the ubiquitous dust of Africa had been stripped away by the furious winds that come rushing down from Mount Kulal, leaving nothing but the blackened bones of old lava flows, like heaps of charred skulls too hot to touch.

Then suddenly, the lake: a sheet of purest jade, bright under dark volcanic peaks, glittering all the way to the farthest horizon. Its waters are long and narrow, stretching north for 180 miles to Ethiopia. To the east there is nothing but the Chalbi Desert; to the west, the bandit-ridden badlands adjoining Uganda.

The first explorer to reach the lake was the Austrian Count Teleki von Szek, in March 1888. He called it Lake Rudolph, in honour of the Crown Prince of Austria; but when Kenya became independent it was renamed Turkana, after the tough, desert-dwelling people who share these northern lands with the Galla, the Boran and the nomadic Rendille.

There is a lodge at Loyengalani, by the south-eastern shore, whose tepid pool offers some relief from the unrelenting heat. When I first went there in the mid-1970s it was run by a glamorous Italian called Isa Barini. There is something about East Africa which seems to attract the solitary, the courageous and the extrovert, and Isa was all three. A jeweller in Italy, she had come to Kenya as a tourist, fallen in love with Loyengalani and sold up everything to buy the lodge. 'Of course there are times when I miss Italian food and the company of people who speak my own language,' she told me. 'But the only thing I cannot live without is Italian music; and when I am really lonely I go to my little hut on the beach and play my opera tapes.'

With Isa at the wheel of her Land-Rover and *La Traviata* blasting at full volume from the speakers, we set off at top speed along the lake shore to look for crocodiles and meet the El Molo tribesmen who live by fishing and grazing their cattle on weed dredged from the water. And like every visitor to Loyengalani, I went fishing for Nile perch. In less than ten minutes I hooked and landed a fish a yard long, a magnificent green and silver creature covered in scales as big as Kenya shillings. To me it was a catch for the record books;

but by Turkana standards it was a tiddler. The boatman did not even bother to weigh it.

Ashore again, the heat seemed more unbearable than ever. Lake Turkana is acknowledged to be one of the hottest spots on earth; a pitiless place with a heart of stone. It was October. No rain had fallen since March; and even then it had rained for only two hours. Yet, for a few fleeting moments on either side of darkness, when the harsh peaks are softened by lavender shadows and long streamers of flamingoes fly along the shores with mournful cries, sunrise and sunset transform this prehistoric inferno into a setting of unearthly beauty.

Chapter Three
Where the Billfish Run

Like faded, blowsy butterflies they came wafting into Mombasa: the great ocean-going dhows of Arabia. Every winter the annual argosy arrived from the Gulf, running before the *kaskazi*, the dry-weather monsoon that blows from December to March.

Laden with Baluch carpets and sweet Basra dates, shark fins, ornate brass-bound Arab chests and salt from Djibouti, they would remain in Mombasa harbour until spring, when the northbound *kusi* blew them home with fresh cargoes of tea and coffee, charcoal, simsim oil and mangrove poles.

That is how it was for a thousand years; but times change. After the Second World War, prosperity born of Gulf oil began to lure dhow crews to less demanding jobs; steamships muscled in on the traditional trade in mangrove poles.

The result was inevitable. In their heyday in the late 1940s you might have seen as many as 200 dhows in Mombasa's Old Port. In 1977, the year I first came to Mombasa, only eight had made the long journey south. 'What we are witnessing,' said Dr John Jewell, author and chronicler of the Mombasa dhow trade, 'is the end of an era.'

One of the first facts I learned from Dr Jewell is that there is no such thing as a dhow. Instead the vessels are called *booms*, *sambuks*, *zarooks*, *kotias* and *jahazis*, depending on their design and place of origin.

Booms are big double-enders from Kuwait and Iran, with an average length of 100 feet. The *sambuk* is a smaller Red Sea craft with a high galleon transom. The scimitar-prowed *zarook* hails from the Yemen, the colourful *kotia* from India and the *jahazi* from the Kenyan island of Lamu.

No two dhows are alike, but all share a common ancestry, the same unmistakable lateen rig, with the mast raked well forward, and the same ancient methods of construction which have hardly changed since the days of Solomon and Sheba.

Dhows are traditionally born on beds of wood shavings and built with Biblical tools: the axe and the adze. The only power tool is a primitive drill which the carpenter twirls with a bow like a frenzied violinist; and the only blueprint is the shipwright's keen eye.

Steeped in oily cricket-bat smells, the hand-hewn hulls take shape, coaxed from crooks of forest teak like the rib cages of Jurassic sea monsters. The only concessions to the twentieth century are drumming diesels instead of tradewind sails, and iron nails instead of the old sewn seams.

One of the people who was feeling the pinch as the dhow trade dwindled was Sharif Mohamed Abdulla Shatry, a former member of the old Kenya Legislative Council, whose family had lived in Mombasa for 600 years. An imposing figure in his long white *kanzu*, he sat in the cavernous gloom of his warehouse in the Old Port, surrounded by Persian carpets, brass coffee pots from Lamu with their distinctive dunce's-cap lids, and brass-bound Zanzibar chests.

'In the old days the carpets would be piled to the ceiling,' he sighed. 'But this year the dhows were half empty. All they brought me were forty carpets and a few chests.'

While waiting in Mombasa for the monsoon to change, the *nakhodas*, or dhow captains, would careen their ships before the homeward voyage, rubbing an unsavoury cocktail of camel fat, lime and fish oil into the hulls to preserve the timber.

Even in the late 1970s it was still possible to negotiate a passage on a dhow. The fare, agreed over small cups of spiced coffee, was around £7 from Mombasa to Lamu, or you could sail all the way to the Gulf for under £300. But this was no luxury cruise. Most dhows exude a rich Billingsgate reek — the ineluctable legacy of their dried fish cargoes. The toilet is a wooden 'thunderbox' slung precariously over the stern and the crew live on a spartan diet of coffee, bread and rice, occasionally fortified with stewed goat.

Today, if you ignore the tourist dhows which ply among the resort hotels of Mombasa and Malindi, the best place to board a sailing dhow is Lamu, off Kenya's north coast.

Lamu is a lazy, laid-back blend of Africa and Arabia; a labyrinth of peeling houses with carved wooden doors, mosques and coffee shops, and shoulder-wide alleys that lead to sunlit squares, to passages and secret courtyards, to rooms within rooms, like Chinese boxes. There are no cars on Lamu. One travels either by donkey or by dhow; and at dusk, veiled women emerge like bats, flitting through the streets in their black *bui-buis*.

In Lamu town I met a man called Obo, said to be the best fisherman on the island, who took me in his small fishing dhow to Manda Island, where we poled along desolate mangrove creeks and waded ashore among fresh elephant footprints to explore the ruins of the lost city of Takwa.

Better still was the visit we made to Matondoni, on the other side of Lamu island. Here, buried in mango and coconut palms, is perhaps the last place in Africa where dhows are built. Even now, local trade remains buoyant enough to keep the Lamu *jahazis* busy, shipping mangrove poles, coral, sand and cement to and from Mombasa, and sometimes farther afield with cargoes of coffee and charcoal for Mogadishu and the Gulf. No doubt, too, in the 1980s, some dhows were used to smuggle poached rhino horn to the Yemen and elephant tusks to the Emirates, where they were carved in secret factories specially set up by the Chinese ivory barons in order to get round the law banning the import into Hong Kong of raw ivory.

Today the Lamu dhows are the last of their kind to grace the Kenya coast. As for the Arabian dhow captains, those sons of Sinbad and their vanished fleets, John Jewell's prophecy proved all too true. 'Soon,' he said, 'the monsoon winds which give them life will seem to blow them out of our minds like a romantic dream.'

Now the great ocean-going *booms* and *sambuks* from Dubai and Khorramshar are only a memory; but down in Malindi the local fishermen still set sail in their local craft: *ngalawas* with crude outriggers.

It was from Malindi that I, too, went to sea with Angus Paul, a young professional big-game fisherman, to hunt the billfish that come in from the deep when the *kaskazi* sets in towards the end of November.

We set out with the early morning breeze at our backs. It blew steadily across the water, carrying the mingled scents of grass, mango trees and warm, wet earth: the smell of Africa. In Kenya they call this land breeze the *umande*, and look upon it as a sign of good fishing.

By the time we reached the blue waters where the big fish roam, the wind would have gone round to the north-east and the monsoon would set in. But for the moment it was still calm inshore, and the local fishermen let out their sails and ran before the breeze. Like us they were heading for the banks and deeps beyond the reefs where the billfish roam.

Our boat, *Tina*, was no primitive local vessel but a thoroughbred 35-foot Striker, built in Holland and powered by Ford Sabre 180 hp twin diesel engines which could push her through the water at 20 knots. Her flying bridge and the outriggers sprouting like long white whiskers from her superstructure immediately marked her for what she was, as did the fighting chair in the stern, where the angler would sit, feet braced against the transom and the butt of his rod anchored in a brass socket, to pit his strength against the giant billfish of the Indian Ocean.

Angus Paul's season begins in November, when the billfish arrive in the 130 miles of fishing grounds which extend down the coast from Malindi to Shimoni. Here they stay, feeding and fattening on the huge numbers of smaller fish — bonito, garfish, Malindi herring — until the south-westerly monsoon sets in during early March and they drift away to spawn, nobody knows where, on their immense and mysterious migrations.

Billfish are nomads, powerful and streamlined, built for wandering the wide oceans. There are five species — swordfish, sailfish, black marlin, blue and striped marlin — each one carrying the distinctive bony beak which is used not to impale its prey but to club it to death with a sideways swipe of the head.

Biggest is the black marlin, which can weigh well over 1,000 lb and hits the bait like a charging buffalo; but at Malindi the most sought-after quarry are the sailfish which gather in large numbers off the mouth of the Sabaki River.

Apart from Costa Rica, the waters here are the best in the world, and most seasons *Tina* averages two sailfish for every trip.

Sailfish are the greyhounds of the sea. They hunt in packs of up to twenty strong, and swim at 40 mph. Everything about them is designed for speed. Even their pelvic fins fold away into a slit in the belly to reduce drag through the water.

They grow to an impressive size, too, though not as big as marlins. The Kenyan record stands at 145 lb; but what brings the big-game aficionados to Malindi is not the weight. It is the sailfish's spectacular beauty, all violet and shining silver, the peacock-blue spots shimmering on its great dorsal sail as it leaps and dances at the end of the line.

Yet for all the numbers of billfish caught, they remain an enigma. 'We still don't know their migratory patterns,' says *Tina*'s owner, Herbie Paul. 'Some think they migrate in a huge circle as far as the Seychelles, but we know only that they come here to feed for four months. Then, for the rest of the year, they simply vanish.'

The Pauls, Herbie and Angus, father and son, are the best big-game fishermen on the Kenyan coast. In 1986 they caught sixteen sailfish between them in a single morning. Herbie, veteran president of the Malindi Sea Fishing Club, was born in Rostock, Germany, sixty years ago, and came to Kenya when he was only six months old. As a young man he worked for a time with the local dhow fishermen, netting sharks for food. Later he tried his hand at sisal farming, but his love for the sea was too strong and he returned to Malindi as a charter skipper, taking clients out after billfish. With his wife Katerina he also runs a small luxury lodge in Malindi, called Kingfisher, and when he is not fishing he is busy with Alistair, his second son, taking people on safari in Tsavo East National Park.

Marlin have always been his favourite quarry. A lot of people ask Herbie to take them shark fishing, but he invariably turns them down. 'I like sharks,' he said, with a twinkle in his piercing blue eyes. Then he turned serious for a moment. 'They've been around a long time. They're the oldest living things in the sea.'

Nowadays he is even losing the taste for billfishing and prefers to let Angus run the boat. 'Big-game fishing is like hunting,' he told me. 'After a while you just don't want to kill any more.'

Angus is different. Lean and laconic like his father, he has a young man's hunger for the thrill of the hunt, the chance of hooking yet another record fish. 'No one on this coast has yet landed a 1,000 lb marlin on rod and line,' he said, 'but they're out there.' Although still only twenty-eight, he was in his eleventh season as a professional charter skipper.

Now, dressed in ragged shorts, T-shirt and yachting cap, he lounged barefoot at the wheel, chatting in Swahili to his crew. Mahomed, the captain, has been with the Pauls for many years. Like Saidi, the deckhand, he is a Muslim, a Bajuni from Lamu, and both men are expert at baiting the wicked two-inch hooks.

The best bait, Angus explained, was fresh Malindi herring or a strip cut from the shiny golden belly of a dorado, the dolphin fish, lashed to the hook and trolled astern with a garish assortment of artificial jigs and lures.

Although I was the only client, we fished with seven stubby glass-fibre rods, each with its metal butt sunk in a socket in the gunwales. To avoid a tangle, the two outermost lines are held up and away from the boat by the outrigggers with the aid of sheaves, tackles and spring-loaded clips. Should a fish strike, the clip releases and the pull of the line comes directly on the rod tip in the normal way.

By now we were off Mambrui, trolling at six knots and rolling like a pig in the uncomfortable swell. The silt-laden Sabaki River, swollen with the November rains, had disgorged an enormous bulge of jade green water extending for five miles out to sea; and it was here, following the distinctive line where the green flood meets the unsullied blue of the true ocean, that the sailfish loved to feed.

Beyond Mambrui the coast was deserted; a waste of sandhills rolling north to Somalia. As the day grew hotter the rising air drew huge cloud castles into the sky. To the west the coral sand beaches of Malindi and Watamu were dazzling in the sun; but inland I could see veils of rain trailing away towards the distant elephant country of Tsavo National Park.

Ahead of us, clouds of terns were hovering, thick as mosquitoes over a lake. 'ndege mingi,' cried Saidi eagerly. 'Many birds.' The birds were a good sign. They hunt the fry driven to the surface by garfish and bonito, which in turn are pursued by bigger predators: sailfish, tuna, wahoo, and kingfish.

As we drew closer the water began to seethe with whitebait and the terns fell upon them in a frenzy. Now I could see schools of bonito feeding, their polished backs rolling in the troughs of the waves as they tore through the frantic shoals.

Without warning a reel began to scream and Saidi was shoving me into the fighting chair. With the butt end of the rod firmly anchored in the socket between my knees, I began pumping in the fish; up with the rod, then lean forward and reel in. I had no idea what was on the other end of the line but it felt as heavy as a horse, and my forearms ached with the strain.

Minutes later, deep down but drawing closer, a dark shape appeared, a gleaming bronze ingot, thickset and curving, with switchblade fins. The rod shook as the fish tugged and twisted with all its strength, but Saidi was quick with the gaff. In a single swift movement it was driven home and the fish hauled over the transom to thump its life away on the teak deck. First blood; a yellowfin tuna, built like a bullet.

There was no time to admire its iridescent mackerel colours. Already Angus was yelling from the wheelhouse and pointing astern where a giant blue fin was slicing through our wake. 'Sail!'

Again there came the unnerving scream of the reel, the same frantic scramble to get into the chair and take the strain. This time the fish dived deep, stripping line in a long, steady plunge that seemed as if it would never end; then suddenly there was no pressure at all.

Had I lost him? I reeled in hard, felt the rod shiver and looked up to see him rising from the water with his huge dorsal fin erect. For a moment, it seemed, he hung suspended in mid-air — all seven feet of him shining purple and silver in the sun — then he re-entered the water cleanly, like a porpoise, his powerful crescent-moon tail going under and the line running out once more.

At last, after an eternity of heaving and winding, he began to tire. I looked into the water and saw the sun's rays lancing down into the cobalt depths, and a huge brown shadow coming slowly to the surface. When he was close enough, Mahomed leaned over the side and grabbed him by his bony bill, then clubbed him over the head and laid him out full length across the deck.

We fished on into the early afternoon, the boat rising and falling among the hills of blue water, the hot sun shining, the terns screaming and dark thunderheads blossoming along the eastern horizon.

From time to time the voices of other charter skippers came over the radio, distorted by static as they chatted to each other like fighter pilots. '*Tina, Tina, Tina*. How's it going? Over.' One boat had just missed a big sailfish which had jumped and thrown the hook. Another had caught a good tuna in the Boiling Pot, a favourite fishing spot off Watamu, where underwater banks cause a violent up-welling of conflicting currents.

But there were no more big fish for us. Only a burnished green-gold dorado, covered in blue spots as if it had just been splashed with ink, and a 9 lb kingfish with bulldog jaws and teeth like razors.

In mid-afternoon we passed a turtle, its polished brown carapace as big as a bathtub, drifting serenely with the current. Sometimes, said Angus, you might see manta rays gliding through the deep on their 10-foot wings, or a whale shark, a gentle, plankton-eating giant bigger than our boat.

As we headed in through a gap in the reef we ran out a red pennant of triumph — the traditional sign of a Malindi boat with a sailfish on board (blue for a marlin, yellow for a shark) — but by now I was filled with remorse for the magnficent fish I had murdered.

I stared at its leathery corpse in the scuppers. How swiftly its quicksilver colours had faded. The dull disc of its cold fish eye, so fierce and glittering in life, stared back at me reproachfully in death. I had not enjoyed the manner of its dying and I wondered afterwards if I was the only fisherman afloat that day who was hoping not to make another strike.

Somehow, size seemed to compound the crime. Killing a sailfish was far worse than catching a mackerel. 'Don't worry,' said Angus, as if reading my thoughts. 'Not an ounce will be wasted. Sailfish is smoked and sold to the resort hotels along the coast. It's a great Kenyan delicacy. And the rest of the catch goes to the locals.'

In Malindi the catch was dumped in a wooden hand-cart and hauled off to be weighed, hung up on a gantry and displayed like the victims on a gamekeeper's gibbet. My sailfish weighed nearly 65 lb: not a bad fish but no record-breaker. I did not mind. I didn't want to pose for a photograph, but I badly needed a beer and wandered off to meet Herbie Paul in the Malindi Sea Fishing Club bar.

The clubhouse lies right on the seafront beneath a barn-like roof of casuarina poles covered with *makuti* thatch. Inside, fans stirred the soupy air that blows straight in from the sea. Herbie poured me a Tusker and pointed to the mounted head of a black marlin, an 828 lb monster caught by *Tina* in 1980. The talk turned to other epic struggles with big fish of the past — the 638 lb mako shark hooked off Shimoni in 1964 which had lunged across the transom in a deliberate attempt to reach the man in the fighting chair — a true-life forerunner of the *Jaws* movies.

It was a tale fit for Hemingway, who fished at Malindi and in the Pemba Channel in 1954 and who has now given his name to a luxury hotel just down the coast at Watamu. Already it has earned a big reputation for blue-water billfishing. Within four months of opening, one of the hotel boats, *Ol Jogi*, achieved the grand slam, one of the rarest events in game fishing, by catching a sailfish and all three species of marlin in a single day.

Gary Cullen, who presides over Hemingways, showed me one of his most prized possessions, a faded copy of *A Farewell to Arms*, signed by the author for his old fishing chum, Colonel 'Benji' Horton. But the game has changed a lot since then, said Cullen. 'In Hemingway's day it was a proper battle. You had to sit there and slug it out with the fish. Now we throw the boat backwards at the fish while you reel, reel, reel.'

Cullen himself was a professional golfer on the major European circuit until a few years ago, when he packed it in to become a fisherman like his father, Anthony Cullen, whose book, *Crash Strike*, is a classic of East African big-game fishing.

'Golf is great,' said Gary, 'but whenever the marlin were running I'm afraid I'd just duck out and head for Kenya. Billfish are so royal, so powerful and dignified and yet so vulnerable. They captivate me. In fact I feel the same as Herbie. I don't much like catching them myself any more, although I love taking people fishing. And even then I find myself hoping that the fish will get away, especially if the client doesn't deserve it.'

Sadly for Kenya, and for the rest of the world, the days of these giant ocean wanderers are numbered. The Japanese, with their long lines and 'wall of death' gill nets, have been plundering Kenya's territorial waters since 1977 to deadly effect.

'They can follow the fish with electronic gadgetry,' said Cullen. 'They can stalk a shoal for days. One Japanese long-liner with 5,000 hooks strung out through miles of ocean can take in a single night what Kenya's entire sport-fishing fleet takes in a year. It's the elephant story all over again. The billfish are vanishing and nobody is listening.'

Later I went again to the seafront at Malindi as the sun was dipping behind the Arab houses of the Old Town. The monsoon breeze had died and the local inshore fishing dhows lay at rest in the shallows with their sails furled.

An odd, dark shape on the sand caught my eye. It was the huge decapitated head of a giant marlin which the fishermen had caught in their nets that day. The carcase had gone to market and the head had been left on the beach for the tide to take away. Now it stood in the gathering dusk with its bill pointing at the African sky while the sea beyond the reef turned to gold and then blood red: a cenotaph for a doomed race.

Chapter Four
Back from the Dead

We drove slowly through Tsavo, the red dust pluming in our wake as we scanned the surrounding bush for movement. Somewhere out in that grey-green sea of thorny thickets were the *shifta*, Somali bandits and ivory poachers. The *shifta* were dangerous, armed with automatic weapons, and we didn't want to run into them.

This was Tsavo in 1988, when parts of Kenya's greatest animal stronghold were considered too dangerous for tourists and placed off-limits as soldiers, police and anti-poaching patrols engaged the ivory gangs in bloody skirmishes that left dead and wounded on both sides. But I went anyway, to report for *The Sunday Times* on the poaching war that was turning Tsavo into an elephants' graveyard of rotting corpses and bleached bones.

My guide was Marcus Russell, a Tsavo fanatic, who had taken his first safari as a three-year-old seated on his father's shoulders. Now, still only in his early twenties, he was leading his own safaris — a tough, dark-haired young man in faded green bush shorts and desert boots. Down on the coast and in Nairobi the word was that Marcus was something of a rebel with a wild streak in him. But in Tsavo, appalled at the carnage he had witnessed, he underwent a kind of conversion and flung himself wholeheartedly into the battle to save the elephants.

With his fluent Swahili and likeable nature he quickly made friends with the local rangers and began to learn something about the web of corruption in which many of the park staff had become ensnared as the ivory rush took off. It was at his direct request that I had come to Kenya to publicise the slaughter of its elephant herds. Marcus knew the risks he was taking, but was convinced that only the pressure of world opinion could end the Tsavo holocaust. Now, together with a wiry little Samburu tracker called Leparowan, we were deep in bandit country.

Inevitably, it was the vultures that gave the game away. Dozens of them, hunched in the leafless trees like obscene fruit. As we drew closer the dry, pure air of Tsavo was poisoned by the gut-churning stench of death.

There were six carcases: an entire family, machine-gunned on its way to water. All had been small elephants and they had fallen where the poachers had surprised them. One had collapsed in a kneeling position, as it lay now, its huge ears still spread as in life, a grotesque parody of an elephant with its trunk chopped off and the tusks hacked out.

I could see the holes where the poachers' bullets had struck. The elephants had been dead only two weeks, but a fortnight in the sun had reduced them to shrunken tents of red hide, splashed with vulture droppings and hollowed by hyenas.

As we drove away a wind blew over the plains, trailing a curtain of rain between us and the Sagala Hills, as if God was trying to cover up the sight of what man had done to His most majestic creation.

Yet even then, amid the butchery, it was impossible not to be aware of the splendour of this harsh land long used to death — the very name Tsavo is a Wakamba word for slaughter — and it was profoundly reassuring to discover that its immense vistas were still vibrantly alive.

The air held that wonderful smell of earth after rain. Golden pipits fluttered up from beneath our wheels, and a troop of oryx, horns glittering in the morning light, cantered off as if they were running for the sheer joy of being alive.

Beauty there was, and wildness and freedom undiminished, but also a sense of tragedy and heartbreak beyond bearing that clung to Tsavo's hills and plains like the taint of an old kill; and the threat of violence remained as strong as ever.

A week later the same gang murdered another six elephants, but this time their luck ran out. As they made for their hide-out in the Kulalu Hills they were spotted from the air by Joe Kioko, the park's acting Head Warden. Within twenty minutes his anti-poaching patrols were deployed. In the ensuing fierce shoot-out which followed, two poachers were killed and another three captured. All were Somalis.

Tsavo is the largest national park in East Africa, an arid wilderness the size of Wales, much of it buried in thick commiphora bush with only an occasional river or distant range of blue hills to break the flat infinity of the plains.

Ironically it was set aside for wildlife only because its sun-stricken thirstlands were of little use for anything else. Yet in a shrinking world and despite years of slaughter by ivory poachers, its 8,000 square miles still hold out the best long-term hope for the survival of a greater number of animals than any other park in Africa: not only elephants but lions, leopards, cheetahs, buffaloes, giraffes, zebras, antelopes and gazelles.

Tsavo's sheer size, although a nightmare to patrol, is ultimately its greatest strength. It is self-sustaining and resilient enough to withstand nature's most devastating blows. What other park could have survived the terrible five-year drought which began in 1970 and killed 9,000 elephants? But in 1988 it seemed as if the poachers were going to finish the herds for good. This was the year when Tsavo should have been celebrating its fortieth anniversary as Kenya's finest elephant sanctuary. Instead the elephants were fleeing from the most savage poaching onslaught in the country's history.

In Nairobi on my way down to Tsavo I had called on Dr Iain Douglas-Hamilton, the world's leading elephant biologist. Iain comes from an ancient Scottish family. One of his warrior ancestors was the Black Douglas, who died in battle in Spain in 1330 on his way to the Holy Land. Iain had first come to East Africa in 1965 as an Oxford undergraduate. He was working for his Ph.D in animal behaviour and had been given a choice: study mice in England or elephants in Tanzania. Needless to say, he chose elephants.

For the next five years he lived in a remote bush camp in Lake Manyara National Park with only a Tanzanian ranger, Mhoja Burengo, for company, trying to recognise elephants as individuals in order to carry out the first systematic study of their behaviour in the wild. It was during this time that he met Oria, who became his wife, and together they wrote a best-selling book about their blissful days in Manyara, *Among the Elephants*.

I had met Iain on my first visit to Africa in 1974. At the end of my stay, with typical Kenyan hospitality, he had insisted on driving me to the airport to catch my plane back to London, and we had remained friends. But much had happened in the intervening years. Manyara had long since been overrun by poachers, and ever since their idyll ended, Iain and Oria had been travelling ceaselessly across Africa, counting its elephant populations and trying to alert the world to the horrors of the ivory holocaust.

More than any other voice, Iain's was the one which would finally persuade the world — with a combination of fierce passion and cold scientific fact — that the harvest of tusks was not sustainable. But in 1988 he was still crying in the wilderness and nobody — least of all the scientists and politicians and conservationist bureaucrats who held the fate of the elephant in their hands — was listening.

Iain was in despair. 'Make no mistake,' he told me. 'What we are witnessing in Africa today is the greatest animal tragedy of this century; and the fate of the elephant will be decided by what happens in Tsavo.'

In 1974 there had been elephants all over Tsavo. Now this vast land appeared utterly deserted. From the Yatta Plateau to Mtito Andei; from Kilaguni Lodge through the Ngulia Valley and all the way down to Mudanda Rock, I saw, not a single elephant. Worse still, there was no sign of their dustbin-size footprints, no green boulders of dung left on the roads to mark their wanderings.

Only an occasional bleached skull, too big even for the hyenas to break open, to hint at the agonies being suffered here.

Not until I left the tourist lodge at Voi and followed the Voi River down to the Kanderi Swamp did I find them. There, miraculously, a herd of about 150 had gathered to feed on the lush swamp grasses. Surprisingly, there were still one or two bulls with good tusks among them; but also an unnaturally high number of youngsters — orphan Dumbos with big round ears and absurdly small trunks — evidence of the large number of mothers and matriarchs which must have fallen to the poachers' bullets.

As I watched, more elephants came striding in from the bush until there were perhaps 350 feeding peacefully. Only here, deep in the park and close to the well-used tourist circuits, did they feel safe.

'Enjoy it while you can,' said Marcus. 'You may never see their like again. You're looking at about 30 per cent of what's left of the Tsavo East herds.' Only last year, he said, he had been seeing herds 600-strong. But the poachers had taken a terrible toll. In the past six months at least 500 animals had been shot, leaving another 300 helpless youngsters for the lions.

We saw no more live elephants that day; but all down the road to the Sala Gate I passed bones and skulls — the poachers had been busy. In Tsavo such victims were known as 'roadsiders' — animals shot from vehicles — the implication being that corrupt park officials were also deeply involved in the ivory racket. But the great mass of killings was almost exclusively the work of the *shifta* gangs.

In Tsavo East during those dreadful days the dead outnumbered the living. In just one small corner of the park I counted thirty-five carcases, each one with its tusks hacked out, all killed in the previous six weeks. One animal, although hit eight times, had managed to hobble away, dragging a shattered leg across 400 yards of rocky ground, only to die within yards of the river it had been trying so painfully to reach. Another, a cow elephant, had been shot in the act of giving birth and lay with her dead calf beside her.

At the same time, in all that immense land, I saw only another eleven live elephants. Among them was a solitary adult female with five bewildered youngsters — all that remained of a 400-strong herd Marcus had seen here only a few months earlier.

It was primarily to protect these huge migratory herds, among the biggest in Africa, that Tsavo was created in 1948. Here the elephants might still wander freely across the vast dusty face of Africa. At least, that was the dream.

But from the very beginning the park was plagued by poachers. In those early days it was the local Wakamba and Waliangulu bowmen — skilled hunters who entered the park to pick off the big tuskers with poisoned arrows. Some of these poachers, like the legendary Galo-Galo Kafonde, were credited with the deaths of many hundreds of elephants, and yet their depredations made little impact until the 1970s.

For years the price of ivory had remained stable at around £1 per pound. But in 1969 prices suddenly tripled and in 1972 they tripled again — almost a tenfold increase in three years. The boom was almost certainly engineered by a few big international dealers and speculators holding back their stocks so that, overnight, ivory became a commodity, like gold, to be salted away in a bank vault as a hedge against inflation or a means of dodging currency controls.

Word spread swiftly to the poachers in the bush, and the ivory rush was on. From Kenya the illegal trade spread rapidly into neighbouring Uganda and Tanzania and then out like some foul disease until it had touched every part of the elephants' range.

By 1974 Tsavo was under siege. The situation had taken a sinister new turn with the arrival of Somali poachers armed with semi-automatic weapons from the war-torn Horn of Africa. The well-organised field force led by David Sheldrick, the park's redoubtable Head Warden, was stretched to the limit but was still in control.

Then, in 1976, the Kenya National Parks Board was merged with the Game Department, a move viewed with deep dismay and suspicion by conservationists — and with good reason. Even then, a whiff of corruption hung about the Game Department. For the smaller but incorrupt Parks Department it was the beginning of the end. Sheldrick was inexplicably removed from Tsavo. He died of a heart attack six months later, and during the chaos that followed the poachers enjoyed a carnival.

One of Sheldrick's last acts as warden was to produce a report on ivory poaching in Tsavo, underlining his concern over the growing power of the Somalis. 'Their sudden appearance in large numbers is almost certainly political,' he wrote prophetically. 'Claiming by right of occupation what they failed to acquire by force of arms, they have infiltrated in large numbers by design and pose a very serious threat in the Tsavo park.'

Just how big a threat was made clear in February 1988 when Iain Douglas-Hamilton organised an aerial count of Tsavo's elephants at the request of Perez Olindo, then director of Kenya's Wildlife Conservation and Management Department. Olindo knew that another dramatic upsurge in the price of ivory had triggered a fresh spate of killings in the park.

The survey confirmed their worst fears. The Tsavo herds had crashed from 17, 487 to 4,327 — a 75 per cent decline since the last major survey sixteen years earlier in 1972.

For conservationists the situation had a depressing air of *déjà vu*. Back in 1975 a major scandal had erupted when the British media revealed that members of President Jomo Kenyatta's family were involved in illegal ivory trading, with the active connivance of some of the highest officials in the Game Department. In 1978, when Daniel Arap Moi became President, one of his first acts was to remove these officials, and for a time it seemed that poaching in Kenya had been brought under control. But in the early 1980s the killing of black rhinos and elephants began again and continued unabated to the point where, in ten years, Kenya lost all but about 400 of its rhinos and 85 per cent of its elephants.

The two questions on everybody's lips were: Who was killing Kenya's elephants? And who was to blame?

In Tsavo there was no doubt that the current wave of poaching was almost entirely the work of the Somali *shifta* gangs — albeit with the help of Kenyan traders in Mombasa and Malindi and the suspected collusion of corrupt officials in the Ministry of Wildlife and Tourism.

Reports of the actual numbers of poachers varied. Some spoke of bandit gangs ninety strong roaming the park, but this was almost certainly an exaggeration. Mostly they operated in groups of from half a dozen perhaps to as many as fifteen, half of them armed and the rest employed to carry out the tusks. Some were ethnic Somalis with Kenyan nationality, but many were from Somalia itself, including army deserters and guerrillas trained in bush warfare.

They moved on foot inside the park, living off the land, extorting money and provisions from villages in the surrounding rangelands and indiscriminately killing animals for food. Only a few days before my arrival a ranger patrol had found a dead giraffe. The poachers had removed its tongue for meat but had left the rest for the vultures.

By day the gangs slept in thickets, leaving a guard up a tree, and cooked only at night when their campfire smoke could not be seen. When surprised by anti-poaching patrols they always made for the hills, where they had their main hide-outs and look-out posts.

At dusk they moved out to follow fresh tracks or stake out waterholes. For the elephants the most dangerous times were the nights of the full moon, when the poachers could operate with impunity, knowing that the park's spotter-aircraft could not take off until dawn.

Ever since the advent of what Iain Douglas-Hamilton has called the 'Kalashnikov Revolution', modern weapons have been cheap in East Africa. The troubles in Idi Amin's Uganda and the endless wars in the Horn of Africa had flooded the continent with surplus guns and ammunition. In 1988 an automatic rifle could be obtained for as little as 500 Kenya shillings (about £17), giving the poachers a clear advantage over the anti-poaching patrols who still had to rely on their old-fashioned Second World War .303s.

Once the elephants had been killed, the tusks were hacked out with axes and hidden in warthog burrows until a big enough cache was ready to be taken out of the park. Then they were carried on foot as far as the main Mombasa to Nairobi road which divides Tsavo in two. There are no fences and the area is so huge that it was easy to make a roadside rendezvous with a middleman — especially since the Somalis also dominated Kenya's long-distance trucking business.

In 1988 the poachers were receiving about £4 a pound for their tusks, depending on the size and quality of the ivory. Although the tusk size had plummeted as the gangs had killed most of the biggest bulls and matriarchs, still the killing went on, with tons of tusks, many no bigger than candles, passing through the hands of Asian and Arab traders in Mombasa, Malindi and Lamu, whence they were smuggled across the Indian Ocean by dhow to Dubai, to be 'laundered' and then legally exported to the Far East as 'worked ivory'.

Top: To heaven in a picnic hamper: tourists take to the air on an early morning balloon safari over the Masai Mara. *(Jonathan Scott)*

Bottom: Jonathan Scott, prize-winning photographer and author of several outstanding books on East African wildlife. *(Jonathan Scott)*

Top: Leopard at Mara Buffalo Rocks in the Masai Mara reserve. *(Jonathan Scott)*

Bottom: The reticulated giraffe of north-eastern Kenya is easily recognised by its distinctive crazy-paving coat. *(Jonathan Scott)*

Big ears, an erect mane and a pin-stripe coat are the trademarks of Grevy's zebra. Kenya's Samburu game reserve is the stronghold of this splendid animal. *(Jonathan Scott)*

Travelling by camel: an ideal way to explore the wild semi-desert country of northern Kenya. Julian McKeand's camel safaris were always accompanied by a colourful team of Laiakipiak Masai. *(Brian Jackman)*

About a dozen big-time dealers were involved, together with a number of smaller operators. Most were known to the police, but these *mafuta mingi* — the 'fat ones' as they were called in Swahili — were also extremely rich and well connected; and although some traders had been pulled in for questioning, none had yet been put out of business.

Throughout 1987 and 1988, increasing numbers of tusks had also been finding their way north into Somalia. There, elephant hunting was banned as herds had shrunk to fewer than 4,000 animals. In 1987 no ivory left Somalia, but reports had begun to circulate suggesting that the country was building up stocks of allegedly 'confiscated' ivory which in fact had been poached in Kenya with the active encouragement of the Somali government.

In June 1988 Somalia announced its intention to export 5,000 tusks, then increased this figure to 8,000 only five months later. Since this represented 4,000 dead elephants — the equivalent of Somalia's entire national herd — cynics could be forgiven for doubting that this was Somali ivory. In fact most of the tusks almost certainly came from Tsavo.

The slaughter of the Tsavo herds and the growing menace of the bandit gangs were bad news for Kenya. The country's thriving, wildlife-based tourist industry is its main source of revenue. Kill the elephants, scare away the visitors and Kenya's economy would lie in ruins.

It was therefore with some dismay that conservationists heard George Muhoho, Kenya's Minister for Wildlife and Tourism, claim improved efficiency in protecting the game. He was speaking at a press conference in Nairobi just two days after Somali poachers had shot dead three rangers in the Kora National Reserve, where George Adamson lived with his lions. Muhoho also admitted that poachers had shot ninety-two elephants in the previous three months (the true figures were much higher) and expressed 'regrets' over the killings, but assured his audience that the affected areas were safe for tourists.

This was too much for Richard Leakey, the distinguished palaeontologist who was Chairman of the East African Wildlife Society. Two days later he unleashed a furious attack on Muhoho's failure to contain the poaching, accusing his ministry of 'lip service' to the cause of conservation and challenging him to tell the truth about the killing of the elephants.

Next day Muhoho struck back. Why, he asked, should the East African Wildlife Society doubt the figures he had issued, which showed that Kenya still had 22,000 elephants? And he challenged Leakey to name any 'high- or low-ranking person' involved in poaching.

Leakey was not to be silenced. The figure of 22,000, he said, was 'misleading'. At the end of 1988 there were no more than 20,000 elephants in Kenya and possibly fewer. Then he dropped his bombshell. The minister, he said, had already received a confidential list naming people inside his own ministry who were involved in poaching. The document had been presented to Muhoho more than a month earlier and had been gathering dust ever since.

'I am reliably informed that the matter is being investigated by the police and as such it is the minister who should name names,' Leakey declared. 'I know the minister got a copy of the document. I did not get one.'

Muhoho's only response was to denounce Leakey for his 'cheeky white mentality', implying — quite wrongly — that it was only Kenya's whites who were concerned about protecting wildlife.

For Muhoho, a former Jesuit priest and the brother of President Kenyatta's widow, Mama Ngina, it was a disastrous performance. But at least the acrimonious exchange with Leakey had put the crisis on centre stage, sparking off a national debate over the fate of the elephants and the chronic inability of the Ministry of Wildlife and Tourism to bring poachers and ivory dealers to justice.

'How many more rangers must we lose before we realise that the threat affects us and not just our wildlife?' wrote Hilary Ng'weno, Kenya's most distinguished journalist, in the *Nairobi Weekly Review*. 'What should be done is certainly more than the issuing of brave press statements. If it is true, as the government itself admits, that some members of the staff of national parks, game reserves and the game department are colluding with poachers, then they should not only be sacked but arrested and prosecuted for their crimes.'

Meanwhile the poachers were becoming even bolder. In September 1988, a tourist was shot and badly wounded when bandits held up and robbed a safari minibus in Meru National Park; two weeks later, after President Moi had ordered all national park officials to shoot poachers on sight, a truck carrying an eight-man patrol of Kenya's paramilitary General Service Unit was ambushed by fifty armed bandits on rangelands adjoining Tsavo West. In the four-hour-long gun battle which followed, two GSU men were killed and several others wounded.

The following month poachers killed eleven elephants almost within sight of Hilton's famous Salt Lick Tourist Lodge. And in November 1988, in their most provocative act so far, they raided Meru National Park and killed five rare white rhinos.

When President Moi heard the news from Meru it is said that he hit the roof. This time the poachers and their protectors had made a bad mistake. By now ten game wardens and rangers had been sacked and dozens of others hauled in for questioning.

At last the tide was turning. Things had already begun to improve in September when a new man, Joe Kioko, a tough senior warden from Nairobi, was put in charge of Tsavo East. It was this move which brought the Anti-Poaching Unit their first much-needed victory in the elephant war. On 16 November Kioko's men finally caught up with a Somali poaching gang, killing two and wounding three more.

In Tsavo's dry bush country the elephants are the linchpin of the entire ecosystem. They are the architects of the African savannah, opening up the dense commiphora thorn thickets, allowing grasslands to spring up where herds of oryx, impala, zebras and gazelles may graze. As the grasslands spread, the watertable rises, with the roots of the perennial grasses reaching down 20 feet and more to break up the hard pan created by permanent scrub.

Elephants destroy trees, it is true; but they plant many others, carrying the seeds far and wide in their droppings. And wherever they roam, their tusking and mud-wallowing create waterholes where other animals can drink.

With the elephants' demise, the scrub was returning, and with it the tsetse fly, killer of cattle. Seasonal streams were drying up, waterholes disappearing. Even the ancient elephant trails, the oldest roads in Africa, were growing fainter as the bush closed in.

Even if the poaching stopped overnight it would take many years for the herds to recover. Dr Joyce Poole, the American biologist who had been studying Kenya's elephants for many years, had produced some alarming evidence pointing to the collapse of the elephants' social structure. Male elephants do not normally begin to mate until they are at least thirty years old. And since it is the older bulls which carry the heaviest ivory, they had been the poachers' prime targets. When Tsavo's elephants were counted in February 1988, out of more than 2,000 animals, only one was a mature breeding bull.

At the same time, many of the old cows which govern the elephants' matriarchal society have also been killed for their tusks, resulting in leaderless families and orphaned calves.

'These elephants are losing their knowledge of the park, where to find food, water and sanctuary,' said Joyce Poole. 'They are losing their whole culture.' Furthermore, she said, any calf under two years of age which lost its mother to poachers was itself doomed, while even those under ten had only a fifty-fifty chance of survival.

The killing fields of Tsavo had become a microcosm of what was happening to elephants all over Africa, from Namibia to Mauretania and from the Atlantic shores of Gabon to the mangrove creeks around Lamu in the Indian Ocean.

For years the world ivory market had treated Africa as if it were a bottomless pit filled with elephants. Now they had been slaughtered to the point where, if the killing continued, they would be gone in five years. Then the unthinkable would become a reality: a world without elephants.

In 1981 there were still well over a million elephants in Africa; but since then, poaching had reduced them to around 650,000. At the same time, numbers in East Africa had shrunk by more than half, from around 429,000 to perhaps 150,000, with Kenya's herds plummeting from 65,000 to 19,000 and still falling.

But slowly the truth was coming out, that the international ivory market was rotten to the core and that attempts by CITES, the Convention on International Trade in Endangered Species had failed utterly to control the trade and to protect Africa's elephants.

Since 1986, when CITES began monitoring the world ivory trade, only 22 per cent had come from legitimate sources. The rest, equivalent to 89,000 dead elephants, had come from animals killed by poachers.

'In most of Africa the ivory trade has driven the elephant downwards,' Iain Douglas-Hamilton had said to me in Nairobi. 'Too many loopholes allow poached ivory to get into world trade. The whole system is out of control.' Iain was fighting for an international moratorium on ivory trading which would give the herds time to recover, but it was an uphill struggle.

An ivory ban was also the dream of Daphne Sheldrick, the widow of David Sheldrick, who had spent his life trying to protect the Tsavo elephants. Daphne campaigned tirelessly to stop the trade and also ran an animal orphanage on the edge of Nairobi National Park, where she hand-reared baby elephants whose mothers had been killed by poachers. She hoped that one day her orphans might be returned to the wild.

'Every piece of ivory is a haunting memory of a once-proud and majestic animal who was a member of a close-knit and loving family,' said Daphne. 'The elephant is also perhaps the only creature besides ourselves with the ability to understand the concept of death and who has to suffer unspeakable agonies to yield up its tusks for trinkets. That is a high price to pay for ivory and the world should want no part of it.'

That was the situation when I went into Tsavo with Marcus Russell in November 1988. For the elephants of Tsavo, and of Africa in general, it seemed like the end of the trail. I stood on the bald granite dome of Mudanda Rock, staring out across a deserted landscape where, only ten years earlier, I had seen elephants in numbers beyond counting. Stained a rich chocolate red from their mud wallows and dust baths, they roamed the park in their thousands. But since then, most had been shot and the coucals sang their lament along the Galana River, mourning the loss of the wise old giants whose ponderous feet had built the web of winding trails reaching out into the invading sea of scrub.

Yet when I returned again in November 1989, the fortunes of the African elephant and its greatest Kenyan stronghold had both undergone a miraculous transformation.

Much had happened in my absence. In Nairobi in July, President Moi had publicly burned a great pile of tusks worth £2 million in a courageous gesture affirming his country's determination to protect its remaining elephants. As the smoke and flames rose into the sky they sent a signal to the poachers in the parks, that their banditry would no longer be tolerated and that they would be hunted down without mercy.

The crackdown had come not a moment too soon; for the latest aerial survey carried out by Iain Douglas-Hamilton revealed that Tsavo now held no more than 6,500 elephants.

Then, in October, at the CITES meeting in Lausanne, while Iain, Daphne Sheldrick, Joyce Poole, Richard Leakey and all those with the elephant's future at heart waited with baited breath, the world voted for an end to ivory trading — at least until the spring of 1992.

For Tsavo the road to recovery had begun in April, when Muhoho was sacked and Leakey was appointed as Kenya's Director of Wildlife and Conservation Management. One of his first acts was to rid Tsavo of the *shifta* gangs whose presence had turned parts of the park into virtual no-go areas.

'A year ago we were losing elephants at the rate of two a day,' said Leakey, a thick-set man in his mid-forties whose warm smile and easy manner belied a steely determination to succeed. 'Now our daily patrols aren't even finding poacher tracks entering the park. The pressure is off. Apart from one isolated incident a month ago when four elephants were shot just inside the Tsavo East border, we haven't lost a single animal since June.'

Thunder rumbled among the hills. It was good to be back, driving down the red dirt roads of a land I had come to love as deeply as my own, and this time with no fears of a poacher's bullet smashing into the windscreen.

For months the brick-red earth had lain cracked and blistered as Tsavo endured one of its periodic droughts. Every day the sun had glittered on a million cruel thorns, on the quartz pebbles of dried-up rivers and the dry bones of old lion kills.

Now the rains had come like an expiation, washing away the past and replenishing the gasping plains, transforming the ashen nyika scrub into a leafy paradise. Acacias blossomed, cloying the air with honeyed scent. New grasses put out tender shoots and white anthericum lilies sprang up overnight, rushing to complete their brief cycle of flowering and fruiting before the dry season returned.

Ten miles from the little township of Mtito Andei, four hours south of Nairobi on the Mombasa road, I turned down the rutted track which leads to the Tsavo River Camp. When I first came here in 1978 it was no more than a row of faded green canvas tents among the riverside palms. Now, rebuilt and enlarged, with a swimming pool and an open dining room under an airy roof of *makuti* thatch, it had become a favourite hide-out for Nairobi weekenders.

A call across the Athi River brought a boatman to ferry me over the water. Later, after lunch and a short siesta in the shade of my tent, I went game-driving in the boundless bush that laps against the escarpment walls of the Yatta Plateau. Birds squealed and chattered in the sharp sunlight: parrots, golden weavers, iridescent blue-green starlings; and the call of a white-browed coucal spilled from a baobab tree like water bubbling from a bottle.

The track that wound through the tangled scrub was pitted with fresh prints of buffaloes, giraffes, zebras and lions; but I saw only graceful impala and the fleeting shape of a lesser kudu drifting like smoke through the fathomless thickets.

As yet there were no elephants, but I did not mind. The wilderness was mine, private and peaceful, for as long as I wished to stay. Shadows lengthened. Francolins scuttled under the wait-a-bit thorns, shrilling with rusty voices. We drove to the top of the escarpment to watch the sun set behind the snows of Kilimanjaro, then drove home in the dark with nightjars flitting in the beams of our headlights.

Tsavo River Camp is a perfect place to unwind. Next day at dawn I lay in my tent and listened as the bush came alive with a babble of bulbuls and robin chats. Then came the measured slap of bare feet in the dust and a soft Swahili voice. '*Hodi?*' ('Are you there?')

'*Karibu*,' I replied ('Welcome.') The tent was unzipped and an African face appeared, slashed by a dazzling smile. '*Chai, bwana.*' I dressed quickly and sat outside and drank my tea while red-eyed doves crooned like contented babies and vervet monkeys with startling azure testicles shook down shower of acacia pods from the branches overhead.

Very different is Kilaguni, Tsavo's best-known game lodge and Kenya's oldest, built in 1926. Now greatly enlarged, it has become a magnet for visitors to Tsavo West, a lunch-time pit-stop for the safari minibus trade. The waterholes beyond the verandah were deserted except for a ghoulish trio of marabou storks; but still it offered the same incomparable views across the plains to the rolling summits of the Chyulu Hills.

From Kilaguni I drove down into the broad Ngulia Valley past Roaring Rock and on beneath Ngulia Lodge in the hills above to emerge on the Mombasa road. Across the road lay Tsavo East, wilder, vaster and even more remote than Tsavo West. At Mudanda Rock I stopped again to clamber up its wind-worn flanks to scan the bush for elephants; but now that the rains had come, those animals which had escaped the poachers' bullets had dispersed across the park.

The rain had refilled the waterholes and all the way to Voi the plains were alive with the movements of kongoni and Thomson's gazelles. Zebras grazed on the new green grass. Buffaloes rose dark and glistening from their mud wallows, and a leopard which had been sunning itself in the road streaked for cover as we approached.

We reached Voi Lodge as the sun was dropping behind the hills. A solitary impala stood near the road, staring intently into a brush-choked gully where guineafowl were cackling in alarm. I could see no lurking predator; but later, in the small hours, I awoke to the thrilling sound of a lion, and wondered if it was a descendant of the legendary man-eaters of Tsavo whose reign of terror had delayed the building of the Uganda railway a century ago.

Voi epitomises all that is best about Kenya's safari lodges. It clings to the side of a granite ridge with a swimming pool built among the rocks and half of Tsavo at its feet. At night, darting genets emerge to forage in the floodlit garden; and at daybreak the colonies of little swifts that nest under the lodge rafters rush out like an arrow storm to greet the sun.

When the day had grown warmer I sat on the terrace with a cold beer, watching the fat African clouds sailing up over the rim of the earth, and felt as if I had arrived at the edge of the universe. High above me, a coal-black Verreaux eagle hung crook-winged in the breeze; and below and beyond lay nothing but bush, threaded with game trails, dotted with anthills and the flat crowns of acacia trees — the sprawling emptiness of the plains as they must appear to the endlessly circling vultures.

Next day I rejoined Herbie Paul, the veteran big-game fisherman I had met in Malindi, who had invited me to stay at his safari camp on the banks of the Galana River. 'This country is so big you have to drive a long way to find the game,' he said as we cruised across the plains near the Aruba Dam, 'but I can show you a wilder, far more exciting park than the standard minibus safari ever sees.'

He was right. Nearby his sharp eyes picked out two lionesses with pale grey coats, hidden deep in a thicket. Tsavo lions are not at all like the big sleepy cats of the Masai Mara. Uneasy at our presence, they whirled to face us, ears flattened and canines exposed in nervous snarls that warned us to come no closer.

We drove on, heading slowly for the Galana. 'This is hard country,' said Herbie, staring at the desolation of stony plains and broken tree stumps which stretched away in all directions. 'It's good for nothing but elephants. I love it,' he added with quiet satisfaction.

Later, there were more lions, herds of buffalo, a mother cheetah with a single cub, and what seemed like all the wintering swallows of Europe swooping and twittering over the river. And best of all, a small family group of red Tsavo elephants, led by a ragged-eared matriarch with long, thin tusks who was quite happy to let us drive slowly within a few yards of her as she rubbed her backside against a large acacia.

Here was proof positive that Tsavo's elephants had come back from the dead to pick up the threads of their former peaceful existence. Now, if the ivory ban could be maintained Tsavo might yet become what it was always meant to be; a haven for man and elephants together.

Back in camp, showered, refreshed and filled with contentment at what I had seen of Tsavo's rebirth, I watched the sun go down and the pelicans coming in to roost in the trees across the river. Out in midstream a hippo surfaced, then submerged with a luxurious sigh. When night fell with its customary tropical swiftness and the first scops owl began to chirrup under the stars, Herbie's Waliangulu tracker cut two fire-sticks — a softwood base and a hardwood spinner which he twirled between his palms until smoke arose from the dried elephant dung he used for tinder.

It was a scene as old as Africa itself. Out in the darkness the air shivered to the rumble of lions, but we were safe in our circle of warmth as the sparks flew upwards into the vast African night.

Chapter Five
Adamson of Africa

At the sound of George Adamson's voice the big lioness left the waterbuck where she had killed it by the river and padded down the track towards us. 'Arusha, old girl,' Adamson cried, and flung his arms around her neck.

It was an unbelievable sight: the old man smiling, the lioness resting her huge head on his bare shoulder, grunting her pleasure at seeing him again, while Adamson patted her tawny flanks and made little moaning lion noises of his own in reply.

I was sitting in the front passenger seat of Adamson's decrepit Land-Rover. The window was down and all around us were the watchful yellow eyes of Arusha's wild pride. 'I shouldn't get out if I were you,' said George.

I had no intention of doing so, especially as Arusha had now wandered over to inspect me. Her muzzle was still wet with blood from the waterbuck kill and I could smell her warm breath as she stared at me through the open window.

That was in January 1980, the day after the funeral of George's wife, Joy Adamson, in Nairobi. Scarcely two months had passed since I had met her for the first time at her camp in the Shaba National Game Reserve. There she had been working on her latest book, about a hand-reared leopard called Penny, whom she had returned to the wilds of northern Kenya. Now she was dead, murdered by one of her former camp staff.

When I had last seen her she was nearing her seventieth birthday. One leg was encased in plaster — the result of a fall which had smashed her knee. Her camp had not long ago burned down when her gas fridge exploded, destroying many of her belongings, including irreplaceable photographs of Penny. Long years in the sun had turned her wrinkled skin to leather, but her hair was still blonde and her blue eyes as clear as when they had first bewitched George back in 1944.

Joy Adamson had the reputation of being a dragon; but when I turned up at her camp unannounced she greeted me with great kindness, sat me down with a beer and talked solidly for four hours about her leopards and how she shared with them a curious kind of telepathy.

She leaned forward in her canvas camp chair, her eyes shining. 'People in Nairobi think I'm crazy,' she told me, 'but I have this gift. Penny and I can communicate. I know what that leopard is thinking.'

Joy Adamson's tragedy was that she was good with animals but bad with people, especially her African staff. To those who knew her well it came as no surprise to hear that a young Turkana cook she had dismissed a few months earlier had returned and stabbed her through the heart.

When news of her murder reached the offices of *The Sunday Times* in London, I was sent to Nairobi to cover the story, and it was there that I met George for the first time. Chatting together after the funeral, I told him how I was working with Jonathan Scott on a book about the Marsh lions of the Masai Mara. Then, out of the blue and with the generosity of spirit which is so often encountered in Kenya, he invited me to his remote camp in the Kora Reserve. 'Why don't you come up and see my lions?' he said. 'I'm flying back tomorrow morning and there's a spare seat if you want it.'

When we landed the first thing he did was to load up his Land-Rover with camel meat and look for his lions along the banks of the Tana River; and it was there that I watched the extraordinary reunion between George and Arusha.

When I returned a year later Arusha was missing. The moment George had worked for — and dreaded — had come six months earlier, when she had chosen to lead her pride across the river and out of the reserve. She was still wearing a telemetric radio collar when she left, but by now the batteries were exhausted and George had been unable to keep track of her.

Worse still, stock had been killed, and Arusha had last been seen with a spear wound in the hindquarters. By now, George reckoned Arusha and her pride might all have been killed. But still he went out every day in his Land-Rover, searching, calling, scouring Kora's dusty game trails for any sign that his lions were still alive.

George Adamson came to Kenya from India well over half a century ago to work on his father's coffee farm, but never took to the farming life. As he put it, 'One coffee bean looked much like another.' He embarked instead on a more colourful career, hunting for ivory, panning for gold, trading beeswax and at one time even delivering milk in old whisky bottles before finding his true vocation with the Kenya Game Department in 1938.

After a spell of active service with military intelligence during the Second World War, he returned to East Africa to resume his job as a game warden, shooting man-eaters and pursuing ivory poachers in Kenya's wild Northern Province.

Then came two events which were to transform his life. In 1944 he and Joy were married; and in 1956 — having had to shoot a man-eating lioness — he found himself with three orphaned cubs on his hands. The smallest was a female. The Adamsons called her Elsa.

So began the extraordinary story of *Born Free*, which brought international acclaim for Joy, but led George down a different road, to Kora, where he devoted the rest of his life to the high-risk business of returning lions to the wild.

Born Free, the story of Elsa, her eventual release and untimely death in Meru

National Park, made Joy a wealthy woman. She followed up its success with *Living Free* and *Forever Free*; and together they sold over thirteen million copies. But fame also brought pressures. Life for Joy became a treadmill: more books, more films, more articles and interviews. Typically, she gave almost all her publishing royalties to the Elsa Wildlife Appeal.

Through all this George stayed quietly in the background, out of the limelight that Joy attracted. And inevitably, their relationship suffered. Joy had many fine qualities but she was not always easy to live with. George was her third husband — she had previously been married to an Austrian, Victor von Klarwill, in 1935 and, after a divorce, to Peter Bally, a Swiss botanist, in 1938. That marriage, too, had been dissolved, and even her closest friends described her as 'imperious and abrasive'. Others, alluding to her numerous marital indiscretions, called her the 'man-eater of Meru'.

In the end the Adamsons separated, amicably, after twenty-six years of marriage. Much affection remained on both sides, and Joy loved to spend Christmas with George. But from then on their ways diverged. Joy went off to work first with cheetahs, and then to return the young leopard called Penny to the wild in Shaba, while George went back to the bush with his lions.

Tired of the bloodletting which his profession demanded, he had retired from the Game Department in 1963. Ever since the idyllic days with Elsa in Meru he had become increasingly fascinated by the big cats and their complex social behaviour; and in 1970, when he and Joy parted, he took off for Kora, saying that he considered his work with his lions was more important than his marriage to Joy.

When you first landed at Kora, stepping out of the plane into the hot desert wind was like standing under a giant blow-drier. The airstrip lay about a mile from Adamson's camp, and the first thing that caught your eye was a notice nailed to a tree. 'LIONS ON ROAD,' it warned. 'BUZZ CAMP AND WAIT.'

For much of the year Kora is scorched by drought, its rust-red earth overlaid by a thorny sea of silver-grey bush in which bald granite hills appear to float away on the quivering air. It is hostile, bandit-ridden country, shared by six-inch-long scorpions and burrowing vipers; but also hauntingly beautiful, and possessing in the Tana River a permanent green artery of shade and water for hippo, elephant, kudu and lion.

'I chose Kora because it was the only place where I was allowed to bring my lions,' George told me. 'It was a sort of no-man's land that no one really wanted.' He rented it from the local council — £750 a year for 500 square miles of wildest Africa.

When he first arrived with his brother, Terence, there were no roads of any kind. But Terence was a compulsive road-builder, and Kora now has 300 miles of tracks, all of them hacked out of the virgin bush, using only hand labour.

Adamson called his new home *Kampi ya Simba* — Lion Camp. It lay just two miles south of the Equator and it quickly became a kind of inside-out zoo where the lions roamed wild and Adamson and his staff lived inside a wire compound. Within the wire stood a cluster of tents and a Land-Rover donated to George by Professor Bernhard Grzimek, Director of the Frankfurt Zoological Society and author of *Serengeti Shall Not Die*. In another corner, an old Mercedes Saloon which had once belonged to Tom Mboya, the dissident Kenyan politician, lay rotting under a spatter of guineafowl droppings.

Life at Kora was simple but never dull. Even visiting the *choo* (lavatory) was an adventure. The camp latrine consisted of an upturned elephant's jawbone strategically balanced on two planks above a narrow pit.

The heart of Lion Camp was the mess room, an open-fronted dining hut with a thatched roof supported on wooden poles. The hut was festooned with all the paraphernalia of life in the bush: Tilley lamps, torches, binoculars and miniature white horses — each one a souvenir taken from the numerous bottles of George's favourite whisky which always appeared at sundown.

There were shelves of books on African wildlife, a two-way radio to keep in touch with Nairobi, two ancient gas fridges and a strong-box containing George's rifles. Above the table and its canvas-backed mess chairs, blown-up photographs of George and his lions stared from the ceiling.

Not all the wildlife lived beyond the wire. Over the years George shared his camp with a multitude of creatures. Ground squirrels begged for peanuts. Yellow-billed hornbills hopped among the dinner plates, snapping up leftovers. Crikey and Croakie, a pair of fan-tailed ravens which bred on Kora crags, dropped in for tea. Bourne and Hollingsworth, a couple of hooded vultures, sat on the perimeter fence, and a two-foot-long monitor lizard known inexplicably as Guildford slept in the thatch.

Sometimes there were less welcome visitors. One day during my stay a large cobra dived down a hole underneath the vegetable cupboard, and George got rid of it by casually poking a shotgun down the hole and giving it both barrels.

But it was the lions, and George's extraordinary rapport with them, which made Kora so special. They arrived from the most unlikely sources. Boy had starred in the film of *Born Free*. Christian was a fifth-generation zoo lion born in Ilfracombe, Devon, who came to Kora via Harrods and a Chelsea furniture shop.

Within a year, George's pride had increased from three to eight lions and it was clear that he would need an assistant. It was then that help arrived out of the blue in the guise of a young Englishman called Tony Fitzjohn, who had thrown up his job delivering milk in London and hitchhiked his way down to Kenya. He had just one ambition — to work with animals — and to George's delight he turned out to be a natural with the lions.

Fitzjohn was tough and capable. He could strip down a Land-Rover, mend a radio; and he was totally devoted to 'the Old Man', although not everyone took easily to Fitz's wild nature. The difference between the two men was enormous; the diffident, contented old patriarch and his restless, extrovert heir apparent. Said Fitzjohn: 'Put it this way. If George is General Custer, then I'm Billy the Kid.'

Meanwhile, the lions of Kora continued to increase. Two of them, Lisa and Juma, had produced their first litters, and when Lisa mysteriously disappeared, Juma adopted her cubs. By now, Christian had been completely returned to the wild and was hunting for himself. George Adamson reckoned it took up to two years to rehabilitate a lion deprived of its parents. 'In that time,' he said, 'it must learn to hunt in the wild and be prepared to fight for its territory.'

The lions began their rehabilitation programme in a wire compound adjoining George's own living quarters. Here, with infinite patience, George and Tony would set out to win their trust. Once the lions had learned to accept their human foster-parents they were allowed out on accompanied walks in the bush.

As they grew older the lions were free to come and go as they pleased, sometimes disappearing for days on end as they explored their strange new wilderness home, though they were still dependent on the camel meat which George always provided out of his slender income. Only when they had learned to hunt for themselves could they be truly regarded as having been habituated to the wild.

The biggest threats to the entire programme were the wild male lions already living in the Kora Reserve. At least two of George's growing pride, including Mona Lisa, were killed by them. There were other tragedies, too. An orphan cub called Katania was killed by a crocodile. But the pride continued to expand. During 1974 there were four new arrivals. Gigi and Growlie came from the Nairobi Animal Orphanage. Fred was a four-month-old cub from Garissa. The fourth newcomer was a six-month-old cub from Rotterdam Zoo. This was Arusha.

As Arusha grew to maturity she quickly became the dominating personality at Kora. She was by far the biggest lioness and in time she became the pride matriarch. Yet both Tony and George agreed that she was always the easiest of all the lions to handle.

Inevitably, however, there were accidents; and George, Terence and Tony all had the scars to prove what a dangerous business they were involved in. In 1975 one of Juma's offspring, a young male lion called Shyman, inexplicably attacked Fitzjohn and bit him through the neck. At this point an extraordinary thing happened. Another lion ran forward and snarled at Shyman, keeping him at bay until George arrived. By this time Fitzjohn was bleeding badly. 'Am I dying, George?' he whispered. 'Yes, I think you probably are,' said George, 'but I'll do what I can.'

Fortunately for Tony the Flying Doctor arrived in time and he survived;

but it was Fred, the young male lion from Garissa, who had almost certainly saved his life.

One evening George told me of his own lucky escape in 1978 when he was attacked by Suleiman, a two-year-old male lion. 'Suleiman and his sister, Sheba, appeared while I was out walking in the bush. They were in a playful mood. While I fended off Sheba in front, Suleiman grabbed me from behind and knocked me to the ground. I tried to beat him off with my stick, but this only made him angry. He began to growl and sink his teeth into my neck. Fortunately I was wearing a revolver, which I seldom carry. I was able to draw it with the idea of firing a shot over his head to scare him off, but it misfired. I fired again — another misfire. Then I got off two shots, but they had no effect upon Suleiman except to make him bite harder. In desperation I reached over my shoulder and shot him. Immediately he let go, walked away a few paces and sat down next to his sister, looking a little startled. By this time I was bleeding profusely but managed to reach the camp, where Terence was able to contact the Flying Doctor and get me patched up. Next day, Suleiman turned up looking little the worse for wear except for a bullet lodged under the skin of his shoulder. But soon afterwards he was killed by a hippo.'

In a way, the death of Suleiman was a relief, for it spared George the agony of having to shoot him, as he had to shoot Boy in 1971. At that time George had an African assistant called Stanley. 'I'd told him never to go out of the compound alone, but he'd gone out to look for wild honey,' said Adamson. 'When he saw Boy coming he panicked and ran. It was the worst thing he could have done. Boy ran after him and grabbed him and I realised, damn it, that I would have to shoot him. I shot Boy through the heart and carried Stanley to my hut; but he died soon after, bitten through the jugular vein.'

On Boxing Day 1978, Terence Adamson nearly met the same fate. He had walked out of the camp only a few yards and stopped to light a match. Crouching down to protect the flame from the wind, he never noticed the young lion called Shade creeping towards him. 'There was suddenly a yell from my African staff,' said George. I looked round and saw Shade walking away from Terence. He had been badly bitten around the face and was damn lucky not to have been killed.' Soon after this incident it was decided that the lion programme should be wound down, though George continued to remain in close contact with his lions, going out regularly to provide them with hunks of camel meat.

A dispassionate observer at that time might have counted the cost and asked what had been achieved at Kora. One African was dead. The Adamson brothers and Tony Fitzjohn had all received bad maulings. Some of the released lions had been promptly killed by hippos, crocodiles and wild lions. Others had simply disappeared, almost certainly shot, speared or poisoned by the Somalis.

But George stuck doggedly to his belief that it was possible to raise orphaned lions and return them to the wild. In spite of the mauling he had received from Suleiman, his trust in the big cats remained unshaken. He had accomplished what no man had done before. He could point to Kora and show the world a man-made pride of wild lions living free. Altogether, by the beginning of the 1980s, seventeen lions had been brought to Lion Camp. Between them they had produced twenty-two cubs, many of them sired by the wild resident males of Kora. That was the measure of George Adamson's triumph. But the tragedy of Kora was only just beginning.

Ever since he had arrived in 1970, Adamson had dreamed of transforming Kora's arid wilderness into a game reserve that would be the equal of Meru, now one of Kenya's finest national parks, where Elsa had made her home and where she now lay buried under a simple cairn. At that time the 500 square miles which George had secured still teemed with game. There were giraffes and zebras, impala, waterbuck and lesser kudu. Elephants by the hundred roamed beneath the Tana River poplars or dug for water in the winding luggas. Rhino slept in the mswaki thickets and leopards lay in their lairs among the red rocky hills.

But even as Kora was officially gazetted as a national reserve in 1974, poaching was bleeding the game parks dry. When the ivory was exhausted it was the turn of the rhino, whose horns were packed off by dhow to North Yemen, to be made into dagger handles. Next was the leopard, poisoned by cattle-dip chemicals. Even the dik-dik, an antelope no bigger than a hare, was gunned down for its inch-long horns.

By now Adamson had become thoroughly disenchanted with mankind and its destruction of his beloved Kenya. It was man after all who had, as he put it, 'killed ten of my lions and murdered my wife'.

Above all it was the constant poaching and encroaching of the Somalis which enraged him most. 'The Somalis are the most destructive people on earth,' he said. 'They've turned their own country into a desert and a battlefield and they'll do the same in Kenya if they can.'

George's presence in Kora was a thorn in the Somalis' side. In 1981 he received a tip-off that a *shifta* gang was planning to ambush him. He radioed for assistance and armed patrols of the Anti-Poaching Unit swept the area for two months.

For a while Kora was secure again; but later that year a Somali gang led by a notorious bandit called Abdi Madobe attacked the remote township of Garissa, killing four government officials. Fearing for George's safety, the authorities in Nairobi suggested that he should leave Kora; but of course he refused. 'I told them the only way they would get me out would be in handcuffs,' he said. But from then on he slept each night outside his hut beside a freshly dug slit trench, which he described dismissively as his 'funk hole'. The idea was that if the *shifta* came for him in the night, he would grab his rifle from under his bed, roll into the trench and shoot them.

By 1984, Adamson's eyesight had begun to fail, necessitating a trip to Europe for a cataract operation. He stayed with Bill Travers and Virginia McKenna, the stars who had played the parts of George and Joy in the film version of *Born Free*, and who had remained among his closest friends; but all the time he was away he worried about his lions. Already, at least another two had been poisoned by local tribesmen who regularly invaded the reserve, denuding the grazing with their flocks and setting fire to the beautiful doum palms which grace the banks of the Tana River, in the mistaken belief that they harbour tsetse fly.

These were hard years for Adamson. At times it must have seemed as if his world and everything he had strived to achieve were crumbling around him, and he mourned for the elephants whose rotting carcases, stripped of their tusks and splashed with vulture droppings, littered the bush in the wake of the poachers. But still he continued to preside over Kora; a leathery figure in shorts and sandals, with kindly eyes and a gentle chuckle, a Buffalo Bill beard and an appropriately leonine mane of silvery hair.

His needs were few: his pipe, a whisky when the sun went down, and the sound of his pride grunting under the African stars. He had made his peace and was ready to meet his end when it came. 'I'm not frightened of croaking,' he once confided. 'Just so long as they bury me here in the bush.'

By 1988 he was more isolated than ever. Two years earlier, the Kenyan authorities had decided that they could no longer support the Kora leopard project which he and Tony Fitzjohn had begun after their work with the lions had ended. Tony, for so long George's right-hand man, had left the reserve to begin a new project of his own at Mkomazi in Tanzania, involving cheetahs and wild dogs. That same year George's brother Terence died. Yet I still received a cheerful Christmas card from George. It showed him sprawled in a camp chair, wrapped in a *kikoi*, smoking his pipe and reading a copy of *The Sunday Times*. Inside the card, scrawled in his frail, spidery handwriting, was the message 'It's a great life in the bush!'

On 3 February 1989, the wild guineafowl that wandered around the Adamson camp were startled by the sudden pop of champagne corks. George Adamson, the grand old man of Africa, was celebrating his eighty-third birthday at Kora, the wildlife reserve which had been his home for nearly two decades.

The champagne, kept nicely chilled in the ancient gas fridge alongside his snake-bite serum, had been specially brought to Kora by friends from Nairobi, a seventeen-hour drive away. But Adamson's most precious gift had arrived the previous November — a trio of lion cubs presented by Perez Olindo, then Kenya's Director of Wildlife and Conservation Management.

The cubs had come from David Craig's ranch at Lewa Downs on the other

Above: Herbie Paul, veteran president of the Malindi sea fishing club and owner of Kingfisher Lodge. *(David Coulson)*

Left: The pride of Malindi: the magnificent mauve-and-silver sailfish, which can swim at 40mph and weigh up to 145lb. *(David Coulson)*

Above: Shopping, Lamu style. Lamu Town is a traffic-free labyrinth of narrow lanes and secret courtyards hiding behind its long waterfront. *(David Coulson)*

Right: Carved wooden doorway on the Kenyan island of Lamu, a lazy, laid-back blend of Africa and Arabia. *(David Coulson)*

Above: The ivory pyre. Elephant tusks and other trophies ready for burning in Nairobi at the orders of Kenya's President Moi. *(David Coulson)*

Left: Up in smoke goes a fortune in confiscated ivory worth £2 million. The message was unequivocal: no more poaching.
(David Coulson)

Top: Tsavo bull elephant; one of the lucky ones that managed to avoid the poaching holocaust. *(David Coulson)*

Bottom: On safari in Tsavo East with Malindi fisherman Herbie Paul, who also runs a small private camp on the Galana River. *(David Coulson)*

side of Mount Kenya, where their mother had been shot as a stock-raider. Only when she had been killed did they discover she was heavy with milk. A search soon revealed three orphan cubs, barely a week old. Without their mother they could not survive — unless George Adamson would agree to take them. So, wrapped in a blanket, they were flown to Kora where they emerged mewling and blinking, to meet the bearded old patriarch who would become their new foster-parent.

For George, separated from Joy for eighteen years and widowed for eight, the cubs' arrival was a poignant moment, re-awakening memories of Elsa, the lioness who had begun it all.

The cubs' arrival seemed to give George a new lease of life. The *shifta* who had long ago vowed to kill him were active again. Only a month before the cubs arrived three rangers had been shot dead less than a mile from Adamson's airstrip. Fearing for the old man's safety, the authorities had tried yet again to persuade him to leave; but he would not budge. So every evening he wound up the brass carriage clock given to him by his father, put his revolver under his pillow and settled down on his trestle bed beside his slit trench.

Kora is one of the loneliest spots on earth; and yet George was never alone. In Africa, where age commands respect, he was venerated as a *m'zee*, a wise old man; but he was much more than that to his staff, who loved him like a father for his quiet ways and kind manners. Abdi, his tracker and driver, was still with him as was Hamisi Ferah, his sixty-year-old Sudanese cook who, for thirty-years, had coaxed miraculous meals from a kitchen consisting of little more than a few blackened pots and a bed of hot ashes. In addition Kora continued to receive a constant stream of visitors: friends, film crews, various celebrities and hangers-on, and numerous pretty girls whose presence — always in the most innocent and platonic terms — greatly pleased the old man.

And of course there were always the lions: Growe, the oldest, now twelve years old; her three adult cubs; six small cubs and the rest of the pride, all third or fourth generation Adamson animals, able to fend for themselves but still fed regular hand-outs of camel meat by the man who could not bear to lose contact with his friends.

It was touching that Adamson should love the animals who on two occasions had mauled him so badly that he might have died. Yet such encounters seemed only to bind him closer to the cats who had come to dominate his life.

It was sometimes said, by scientists and conservationists who criticised his work, that he had not advanced man's knowledge of lions. They were forgetting that perhaps what he had discovered told us more about ourselves. Deep down Adamson believed in the unassailable dignity of wild lions. 'Their code of behaviour is worth our respect,' he wrote in his autobiography, *My Pride and Joy*. 'Indeed, some of their genetic commandments look no worse than ours and are more often heeded. Self-reliance and courage; tenacious yet realistic self-defence of a realm; the willingness to care for the young of another; brotherhood, loyalty and affection are seven commendable precepts.'

Above all, George could not bear to think of a lion that was not free, as if he, too, hated the thought of a life shut up in the busy streets of Nairobi or London. He enjoyed his occasional visits to civilisation, seeing old friends such as Bill Travers and Virginia McKenna; but after a while he would fret for the bush where he belonged, among the lions he mostly preferred to people.

The day of his birthday party went well. He had fully recovered from the cataract operation and was in great form. Unfortunately, the birthday cake which the photographer David Coulson and his friend Doddie had brought from Nairobi had suffered on the long drive. The icing had melted, but they stuck a few candles on it and drank the champagne while George regaled them with the latest exploits of Growe and her pride.

He was clearly delighted to be sharing his day with the three cubs — the first to be reared at Lion Camp for a decade. He had named them Batian (after a famous Masai *laibon* or chieftain), Rafiki (friend), and Furaha, meaning joy. When Abdi carried the champagne bucket into the cubs' enclosure they were intrigued by their reflections in its shiny surface.

Later, as the sun went down, George stood with his loud-hailer and called to the wild lions outside the wire to come and join the celebrations. His frail voice, given strength by amplification, echoed among Kora's blood-red cliffs as it had of old, causing the lanner falcons to scream in their eyrie and the guineafowl to cackle in alarm. 'Come on Growe, come on Dennis, come on Maggie.' His words boomed into the deepening dusk, audible two miles away. Some time afterwards, during supper, David Coulson remembers hearing a rustle outside the wire. 'I flipped on my torch,' he says. 'It was the lions. They had answered George's call.'

After the party, David and Doddie went back to Nairobi. The months passed. The *shifta* continued their murderous attacks until not a single elephant was left alive in Kora; but down in Nairobi the tide was turning. Richard Leakey had taken over the anti-poaching offensive and begun the battle which would eventually clear the bandits from the parks.

The three cubs, meanwhile, were growing fast in Adamson's care. They would not lose their milk teeth until they were fourteen months old, but already they accompanied him on walks into the bush as of old, following the dirt roads Terence had built.

Adamson walked more slowly now, with the aid of a stick; but he could still climb Kora Rocks as he had with all his other lions, with Boy and Christian and Arusha, so many years ago. Those were among his happiest days, and he loved the cubs for re-awakening those treasured memories.

Friends who had visited him in early August were amazed to find the old man in such fine form. He had been poorly after a bout of pneumonia but seemed to be fully recovered. The short rains had come unseasonally early to Kora, bringing a flush of fresh grass and the marvellous smell of slaked earth. The acacia trees burst into blossom and weaver birds had begun to build their nests.

Down south, Leakey's men were cracking down on the *shifta*. Thirty poachers had been shot dead and the last of the gangs were on the run. And better still, news had just reached the Adamson camp that at last, after nearly twenty years of struggle, Kora was to be made a national park. Although Kora was a game reserve it was still perfectly legal for semi-nomadic Somali Lerdsmen and other local pastoralists to graze their stock inside its boundaries. By receiving national park status Kora would at last become a true wildlife sanctuary where conservation was paramount and all human activities except for wildlife tourism would be forbidden.

George was delighted. Now only one worry continued to nag him. For months he had seen and heard nothing of the wild lions. But then, on 19 August, the strangest thing happened. That evening, after his regular sundowner, the entire pride had gathered around Lion Camp, grunting and roaring all night long. It was, said his friends, a magical moment which the old man found inexpressibly moving.

That night he went to bed more contented than he had been for weeks, thrilled that Growe and her pride were still intact. The next day he was shot dead by three Somali bandits as he drove out with his revolver in his hand to rescue his driver, Abdi, and a German guest.

A plane had arrived at noon with four guests, buzzed the camp and then landed at the airstrip to wait for transport. Walking through the lion-infested bush was positively discouraged. When George heard the plane he sent Abdi and a German friend, Inge Leidersteill, to meet them, but they were ambushed about a mile from the camp. Shots were fired. The bandits demanded money, broke Abdi's legs with an iron bar and badly beat Inge. Back at camp, Adamson heard the shots, gathered three of his staff and drove at top speed to the rescue in his back-up vehicle, a Land-Rover whose battered sides bore the slogan 'All aboard the Nightingale'.

The bandits, armed with G3 automatic rifles and an AK-47, were waiting for them. When the Nightingale appeared, they opened up with a volley of shots. One of Adamson's men, Mohammed Maru, jumped out of the still-moving vehicle, but George and his two other Kenyan employees drove on to their deaths, after which the killers ran off into the bush.

The eulogies poured in from all over the world. Adamson was a warrior for conservation, an ambassador for wild Africa. 'George Adamson put Kenya on the map,' observed Richard Leakey. 'He was a man of incredible character and dedication who died fighting against people who would harm the wildlife he loved so much.' Hamisi, his cook, wept inconsolably. 'He was a marvellous man,' he sobbed. 'He was getting old and frail. We were like brothers.'

On 2 September 1989, George Adamson was buried at Kora as he had wished, beside the grave of his brother Terence and that of Supercub, one of their favourite lions. A simple cairn — since vandalised by the Somalis — marked the spot.

If I close my eyes I can see him now, sitting under the Tilley lamp with his pipe and his memories, staring into the dark as if the lost continent of his youth was still out there, that old Africa, wild and fresh and innocent, in which nobody could believe that the game would not go on for ever.

He was the most contented man I have ever known, but one spectre continued to haunt him: what would happen to his lions when he was gone? 'Who will raise their voices on behalf of Kora when my own is carried away on the wind?' he asked.

Three days before the wind came for him, his plea was answered when Kora was officially gazetted as a national park.

His death was a tragedy; but at least he died as he had lived, a fighter for conservation, going down with a gun in his hand like the grand old warrior he was. And maybe his death was as merciful as it was quick. For in the end he had become almost as much an anachronism as the vanishing rhino — one of the last of the old breed of bush adventurers.

Today Kora seems strangely deserted. Tony Fitzjohn, the natural inheritor of Adamson's skills, is still in Tanzania, supervising the construction of a new camp in Mkomazi game reserve to continue the old man's dream. The three cubs were given a new home down south in Botswana. As for Growe and her pride, they stayed in Kora, forever free, giving thunderous voice to the 500 square miles of pristine wilderness which is George Adamson's lasting gift to Africa.

Chapter Six
Serengeti Days

Ngare Sero — the 'Place of Sweet Water' — is a comfortable, turn-of-the-century coffee farm at the foot of Mount Meru, just half-an-hour's drive from Kilimanjaro Airport. Converted into a small private tourist lodge by its owners, Mike and Gisella Leach, it is the perfect spot in which to unwind after the long flight from Europe.

The air at Ngare Sero is heady with the sweet scent of frangipani flowers. From the verandah, with its wooden eaves and swallows' nests, you look down to a small lake in the lodge grounds, where trout cruise among the lily pads and weaver birds squeal in the reeds. The lake is alive with water fowls. Towards dusk the resident heron colony comes noisily home to roost in the tall loliondo trees; and it is then, if you are lucky, that you may see the evening sun ignite the unearthly snows of Kilimanjaro, some forty miles away.

In early May I was denied this spectacle because the long rains were still falling. Every evening I sat on the verandah and waited for the summit of Africa's loftiest mountain to appear; but Kilimanjaro remained a mystery hidden in cloud, and I saw only a succession of storms sweeping across the surrounding banana shambas.

Yet there were rich compensations for visiting Tanzania out of season. The days were warm and sunny and the morning mist soon melted away to reveal the great ash cone of Mount Meru, whose thickly forested slopes soar into the sky behind the lodge. Not until nightfall had been announced by the jangling choirs of crickets and tree frogs did the rain begin in earnest. Then, in the stillness of evening, when the cedarwood fires had been lit, I could hear it approaching with a sound like distant surf.

Awaking at daybreak, I would find the whole world green and grey, the grass soaking, the sky overcast. But soon the sun burned through, causing the rich red earth to steam warmly. Raindrops glittered on every leaf and the garden glowed with fresh blossoms brought forth by the overnight drenching: sky-blue morning glories, sprays of golden cassia and the white, waxen trumpets of datura. If Africa could be said to have a springtime, then surely it was now, in this miraculous season of renewal.

Close by, in the forested foothills of Mount Meru, is Arusha National Park. Although small by Tanzanian standards — only 20 square miles compared with the Serengeti's 11,500 — its crater lakes and grassy glades are exquisitely beautiful. Spectacular black and green swallowtail butterflies hovered at the edges of muddy pools. A long-crested eagle stared down from a tree and scaly francolins scuttled through the leaf litter on short red legs.

Animals proved harder to find. Giraffes and dik-dik were quite common but most other species — buffalo, elephant, the copper-coloured bushbuck and shy forest duiker — were no more than fleeting shadows at the edges of the glades and the resident troops of black and white colobus monkeys only an eerie, rasping chorus in the forest canopy.

Even so, the Arusha park is not to be missed — especially the extinct volcano of Ngurdoto which lies in its south-eastern corner. The crater floor measures nearly two miles across and is a true sanctuary where no visitors may enter. From its wooded rim you stare deep down into a pristine amphitheatre of grass and water, where reedbuck browse undisturbed among throngs of storks and egrets.

The following day I left Ngare Sero and set out upon a journey which, I hoped, would fulfil a lifetime's ambition. For as long as I can remember I had longed to make a safari into the Serengeti, to sleep under canvas, to awake to the sound of the famous Serengeti lions roaring their triumphant cadenzas at the dawn, and to witness the greatest wildlife cavalcade on earth, when the wildebeest gather, more than one million strong, to give birth to their calves on the short grass plains.

I had often watched them when they crossed into Kenya, charging across the Mara River in their tens of thousands to feed on the tall red oat grasslands of the Masai Mara National Reserve and fall prey to the Marsh lions.

Often, too, when they returned to the Serengeti in September, trekking south to the short-grass plains and granite kopjes around Naabi Hill, my thoughts had gone with them. There the herds would give birth in the new year; and there they would remain, the greatest biomass on earth, harried by the waiting predators until the end of the rains forced them to move on. This was the spectacle I now hoped to see.

My guide was Baron Hugo van Lawick, whose prize-winning documentaries on the wild dogs, cheetahs, lions and jackals of northern Tanzania have made him one of the world's most distinguished wildlife film-makers. For a quarter of a century, 'Bwana Baron', as Hugo is known to his African camp staff, has lived in the Serengeti, observing its animals through the camera lens.

We had decided to break the journey from Arusha, taking three days to reach the Serengeti in order to see two more of Tanzania's jewels: Lake Manyara National Park and Ngorongoro Crater. Stopping only at the village market in Mto wa Mbu to buy some of its famous red-skinned bananas, we drove on up the Rift Valley escarpment to check in at the Lake Manyara Hotel.

From my bedroom window I could see what looked like a mass of snowflakes turning in slow spirals over the lake's placid surface. They were pelicans, soaring in the thermals that build up in the valley during the heat of the day.

Like the Arusha park, Manyara is small by East African standards. From the main gate to Maji Moto, the hot springs at the farthest end of the park, it is only 25 miles; but the landscape, wedged between the lake and the Rift Wall, is indescribably lovely, with its cool ground-water forest, rushing streams and the grassy flats known as Mahali pa Nyati ('The Place of the Buffalo') reaching out to the lakeshore.

Manyara is renowned for its fleets of pelicans, massed flamingoes and large schools of hippo. It is also known for its tree-climbing lions, which have developed the curious habit of sleeping by day some twenty feet above the ground in the flat-topped *tortilis* acacias.

We failed to find the lions, but spent the afternoon sitting in Hugo's Land-Rover with the engine switched off as elephants began to emerge from the woods. Soon they were all around us, ears swinging like sails becalmed, feeding quietly as they walked.

When one old matriarch strode purposefully towards us and began to sniff at us with outstretched trunk, I cast a sidelong glance at Hugo, but he seemed unperturbed. As the tip of her trunk hovered a mere inch or two from my open window, I looked up to see a brown eye shaded by soft lashes staring down at me. For what seemed like an eternity she loomed over us. Then, assured that we meant no harm, she turned and strode soundlessly away.

Hugo grinned. He was in his element. 'I knew she wouldn't cause us any trouble,' he said. 'If she had meant business she'd have probably charged the moment she saw us.'

In the ground-water forest the air smelled of leaf mould and rang to the flute-like calls of orioles and bou-bou shrikes. Surely, I thought, there could be nowhere in Africa more serene than Lake Manyara? But that was before we reached the lost world of Ngorongoro Crater.

Grinding in first gear up the steep wooded slopes towards the crater rim, we passed cave-like hollows gouged into the roadside banks where elephants had tusked at the red earth in search of mineral salts. Giant *nuxia* trees bearded with lichens alternated with glades of pink-flowering *ernonia* shrubs and the tall, pale trunks of the *cassipourea* trees which clothe the steep-sided gullies and ravines. At one spot, rounding a bend just below the rim, we saw a splendid male lion in the grass beside the road. He stared at us with stony eyes as Hugo stopped to photograph him, but did not move away.

Ngorongoro is the caldera of a long-dead volcano; a giant hoofprint 12 miles across, stamped into the green hills of Masailand. At first, gazing down from the crater rim, you see nothing but sunlight and cloud shadows falling across the crater floor 2,000 feet below. But look with binoculars and the finer details swim into focus: dark patches of papyrus pinpointing the Gorigor and Mandusi swamps, the frail calligraphy of game trails and seasonal watercourses, a pink blush of flamingoes at the soda-crusted edge of Lake Magadi, and a solitary dark speck far out in the grass that just might be a black rhino.

Later, once we had driven down to the crater floor, Hugo told me how he had lived here for two years with Jane Goodall, his first wife, and their baby son; and how he had returned on his own to live there for six months while filming *The Hyena Story*.

Before the First World War the crater was the home of two German farmers. Although they were brothers they never spoke to each other, and lived on opposite sides of the Munge River. Now, even camping is forbidden and all visitors must return to their lodges on the crater rim before sundown. Nobody lives there any more and the crater has gone back to the animals.

In late afternoon the sun slid closer to the crater rim. The long light slanted through the tall grass where two male cheetahs stared at us with agate eyes. They must have killed earlier in the day, for their bellies looked full. Now they were resting, lolling in the grass with nonchalant ease.

Almost certainly they were brothers, young nomads from the Serengeti who had become independent of their mother and then stayed together for mutual protection and co-operative hunting. In the hostile world of the cheetah such coalitions are common, and will invariably fare better than a solitary animal which must fend for itself. Even so, they must have had a hard time among the large numbers of lions and hyenas.

Towards evening we stopped at the edge of the Lerai Forest. Hugo lit a cigarette and I sat on the Land-Rover roof, listening to an oriole calling from the fever trees, while far out in the deepening gold of the crater floor a mother rhino and her calf moved in slow silhouette towards a distant gleam of water.

The night at Crater Lodge was cold, and we sat close to a log fire, drinking beer with Sirili, Hugo's veteran cook, and Renatus, his mechanic. Outside, dew settled on the grass and bull buffaloes wandered in from the cloud forest to graze on the lawns.

Later, an askari dressed in an old army greatcoat escorted me back to my room. He carried a torch in one hand and a spear in the other, and I asked him what would happen if the buffalo should come for us. 'Oh, we just run away,' he said with a disarming smile; but fortunately the docile old bulls ignored us.

When we left next morning, the lodge was wrapped in swirling mist and the crater was invisible. We drove for miles among high, bare hills where cattle bells clanked in the drifting cloud and Masai herdsmen stood wrapped in cloaks against the chill. Once we surprised a leopard, which fled across the road in front of us and vanished into the dripping bushes. But as soon as we began to descend towards Olduvai the mist dissolved and the sun burned fiercely through the roof hatch.

Giraffe were browsing among flat-topped acacias, and beyond, swimming away in the rolling heat, I could see the immense plains of the Serengeti, the great emptiness of grass and sky which the Masai call *Siringit* — 'the Wide Place'.

Anxiously we scanned the horizon, searching for the wildebeest. The rains had been fickle, disturbing the pattern of the migration. Only two weeks ago, we were told, the herds had gone north towards Lobo, near the Kenyan border.

We need not have worried. Lured by the rains, they were back on the short-grass plains in numbers beyond counting. This was how the American prairies must have looked in the days of the bison. On every side, herds of wildebeest — their numbers swollen by cohorts of zebras — stretched as far as the eye could see. To reach Hugo's camp at Lake Ndutu we drove through their midst for fifteen miles, and still there was no end to them.

The camp — someone once called it 'Hugo's Hilton' — is a row of faded green tents shaded by tall acacias on a low bluff overlooking the lake. *Ndutu* means 'the Peaceful Place' and there was never a moment when it did not live up to its name. I shared my tent with a pair of mosque swallows which had built their mud nest under the canvas awning and swooped in and out quite oblivious of my presence.

Over the next few days, as I learned to recognise the silhouettes of distant hills and mountains — Lemagrut, Naabi, El Donyo Lengai — Hugo showed me the hidden corners of his savage paradise. We journeyed far off the beaten track, lurching and swaying in the wake of the wildebeest, to places tourists seldom see, looking for the lions of the Gol pride, whose cubs seldom survive the rigours of the dry season when the herds have departed. Always we kept watch for the wild dog packs which sometimes accompany the migration.

The Genghis pack which Hugo had filmed some years earlier were all dead; but some of their pups could still be alive, and we set out to search for them in the secret valleys of the Gol Mountains. Here we were alone except for the nomadic Masai, whose *manyattas* made thorny circles on the hillsides. Towards evening we pitched our tents at a place called *Kampi ya Menafu*, 'Camp of the Wild Spinach', and listened to the jackals keening in the softly falling dusk.

After supper three Masai walked out of the night and sat with us by the fire. They gave us milk from chestnut-coloured gourds. In return we gave them coffee, but what they really wanted was *dawa* — medicine for their families — and next morning we called at their *manyatta*, where Hugo dispensed *dawa* as best he could from his first-aid chest, to children with eye complaints, men with headaches and women with pains in their stomachs.

The Masai told us that often in the past few months they had seen a pack of six wild dogs, and we drove out to look for them, heading away from the Gol Mountains towards the Barafu Kopjes.

At midday we stopped for a flask of coffee in the shade of a solitary giant fig tree. Clearly there was water here; nearby was an old Masai well, even though we were far out on the plains and there were no other trees for miles.

The fig was enormous, completely dwarfing our vehicle. I measured the root system, which extended for fifty paces from the grizzled trunk, and wondered at its age. Could it once have sheltered the ancient hunters whose stone tools and obsidian chippings we had found beside a waterhole in the Gol Kopjes?

We moved on, scouring each lonely kopje, finding a barn owl's nest in one, and in another disturbing the siesta of a grand old lion — a nomad evicted from one of the up-country prides, Hugo thought. But of the dogs there was no sign.

As we returned towards Ndutu a dry-season wind came blowing over the close-bitten grass. Already the wildebeest had sensed the change and were streaming away towards the Itonjo Hills in plodding columns that seemed to reach to the ends of the earth. They had begun the great migration that would take them west and then north into Kenya, to the lush wild meadows of the Masai Mara which I knew so well, and where the Marsh lions would once again be waiting for them. In the dying light we watched them go, marching westward under banners of dust. Then darkness fell and we could watch no more.

He was an old lion and he lay on the rock with his chin on his paws. The dry-weather wind that had blown since the previous day hissed over the plains from the Gol Mountains, lifting the edges of the heavy mane which fell around his shoulders like a rug; and when he panted, slack-jawed in the heat, I could see that he had lost one of his lower canines.

He was one of the two resident males which together had ruled the Gol pride for the past two years. His brother was sprawled in the grass nearby, guarding the half-eaten carcase of a zebra they had killed in the last hour before sunrise. Now flies had gathered on the zebra's remains, as thick as cloves on a honey-roast ham, and the two lions were resting. Their bellies were full and yet they seemed ill at ease. Every so often the lion on the rock would lift his huge shaggy head and sniff the breeze as he stared with far-seeing eyes across the great emptiness of the Serengeti.

Somewhere out there were his enemies, the lean and rangy nomadic lions which had moved into his territory with the onset of the wildebeest migration and which now with increasing boldness were challenging his supremacy.

Lions lead brief lives. Mature at five years old, veterans at eight, the males may enjoy only a few season's in possession of a pride before they are ousted by younger rivals and cast out to fend for themselves until, worn down by age, hunger and disease, they wait for the hyenas to move in from the shadows.

Such was the fate awaiting the veteran on the rock. Maybe he sensed that his days were numbered, that the seasons of plenty when he sired his cubs and grew fat on the kills provided by his three lionesses were at an end. When the final confrontation came, he and his brother would be no match for the challengers. But until then, this was still his land, his kingdom of the grass.

Serengeti. Even its name resounds like a drumbeat from the heart of Africa. How can one convey the majesty of its immense plains? The light is dazzling.

The air smells of dust and game and grass — grass that blows, rippling, for mile after mile in the dry highland wind, with seldom a road and never a fence; only the outcropping granite *kopjes* and their watching lions, the thorny woodlands, the watercourses with their shady fig trees, and the wandering herds of game.

In the Serengeti, grass is life, and the herds are always on the move, chasing the thunderclouds across the land in search of the green flush which springs up after the storms.

Some animals such as the Grant's gazelle can go for months without drinking. In the dry season, long after the rest of the herds have trekked north into the acacia woodlands or crossed the Mara River into Kenya, the gazelles remain, nibbling at the parched stubble left by the departed herds. But the great mass of plains game need fresh grass and water, and none more so than the ungainly wildebeest.

The wildebeest is the ugliest of antelopes. It has the horns of an ox, the mane of a horse and the sloping hindquarters of a hyena. Yet despite its grotesque appearance and clownish cavortings, it is the most successful of all the grassland animals, dominating the plains by sheer weight of numbers.

Since the Serengeti became a national park some forty years ago, the wildebeest have multiplied until there are now one and a quarter million of them. Together with half a million gazelles, 200,000 zebras, 50,000 topi and 8,000 giraffes — to say nothing of 1,500 lions — they offer a last glimpse of Africa as it was before the coming of the Europeans; and when the wildebeest embark on their seasonal migrations, stampeding across the rivers, stretched out from horizon to horizon in endless marching columns that take three days and nights to pass, there is no more dramatic place on earth than these wide Tanzanian plains.

Surprisingly, for a park the size of Holland, the Serengeti contains only a handfull of tourist lodges. Lobo, in the north, offers a spectacular setting among giant granite boulders, in the kind of country Hemingway described in *Green Hills of Africa*. Seronera, in the centre of the park, is renowned for its airy glades of yellow-barked acacias, its sleeping leopards and large prides of black-maned lions. But Ndutu, on the southern edge of the Serengeti near Lake Lagaja, is the place to be when the wildebeest gather on the short-grass plains.

In a normal year the herds leave their dry season refuge in the Masai Mara in September, drifting through the northern woodlands and munching their way across the oat-grass meadows of the Seronera Valley until they arrive on the open plains in November or December.

This is the season the Masai call *Ilkiserat*, when sudden showers trail across the land, replenishing the sweet, mineral-rich pastures of the short-grass plains which begin at Naabi Hill. Here the herds remain throughout the rainy season, producing their gangling brown calves towards the end of January in such prodigious numbers that the waiting predators — lions, leopards, cheetahs, hyenas and hunting dogs — can never kill them all. Such is the harsh but effective survival strategy which has enabled the wildebeest to multiply.

This January, unseasonally heavy storms had swept the Serengeti. It had rained so hard that several Masai were swept away as they tried to cross a flooded river, and parts of the park were under water. When I arrived at Ndutu three months later, the plains were still green, but drying fast. The wildebeest, their calving season at an end, had begun to stream away, although zebras and gazelles in their tens of thousands remained on the grasslands around the Gol Kopjes.

This was where I had found the old lion and his brother, and it was here that I spent the next two days following cheetahs with Hugo, who knows this country better than anyone.

Hugo had begun shooting a new film on the Serengeti cheetahs, which the migration had lured south to the Gol. The film centred on the fortunes of a particularly aggressive trio of young males, known as 'the Blood Brothers', and two other youngsters: a brother and sister from another litter.

Lions were grunting in the dawn as we set off by Land-Rover with the barrel of Hugo's camera poking through the window like an Armada cannon. As the day came alive, the throbbing chorus of Cape turtle doves echoed through the acacia glades. The air was chill, and the open plains when we reached them were glistening with dew.

To drive out on a bright morning into the deep silence of the plains is to know the solitary joys of the long-distance yachtsman. Adrift in the rolling seas of grass, in the slow rise and fetch of the land, charting a course through the scattered archipelagos of the *kopjes*, I wished I could go on forever, but Hugo had a job to do. A short, stocky figure with a ruddy face and a military moustache, he sat at the wheel in his thick blue sweater, steering towards the northern horizon, where two isolated *kopjes* pierced the infinity of plain and sky. As we drew closer they stood out sharp and clear, their granite flanks gleaming in the hard light, like the hulls of wrecked ironclads.

Islands in the green, each Serengeti *kopje* is a closed and secret world; a watchtower for the hunting cheetah, a refuge for the lionesses who retreat into their dark clefts and caves to produce their cubs. In the treeless void of the short grass plains, only the *kopjes* offer shelter from the sun; but the migrating herds steer clear, fearing the predators that haunt these ancient killing grounds.

We, too, scanned the rocks for the elusive cats, but without success, and drove on to the next ridge to sweep the surrounding slopes with binoculars. To the east, giant cliff-heads of raincloud now towered along the distant skyline. Against them, etched in sunlight, a slender cat stood out in perfect profile.

The cheetah stood quick and golden on the plain, a vibrant, quivering creature, alert and taut with unconcealed hunger. As we approached, another rose up out of a patch of sodom apple and stared at us with unblinking eyes.

They were the brother and sister he had been filming, said Hugo, about fifteen months old and not long independent of their mother. Their bellies were thin — they had not yet killed — and we settled down at a considerate distance to follow them.

Of all the Serengeti animals the enigmatic cheetah with its tear-stained mask and sway-backed racing frame is the true predator of the open plains. Here, with no place to hide, life hangs on the survival of the fastest, and the rakish, loose-limbed cheetah is the culmination of an ancient and inseparable bond between hunter and hunted. It has evolved stride by stride with the gazelles, the slenderness and quicksilver pace of the one matched by the feline grace and devastating acceleration of the other.

Ahead of us, the herds had stopped grazing. Tension crackled across the plain. All heads were up as the two cheetahs strode purposefully towards a throng of Thomson's gazelles, which in turn were drawn towards the cats as if hypnotised. But the haughty cheetahs ignored them. They were looking for the fawns which are easier to catch than the fleet-footed adults.

When none appeared the cheetahs slumped down to rest. The sun rose higher. The day fell quiet. The plains lay drugged with heat.

An hour passed, and then another, but Hugo was perfectly content to sit and wait. So long as he had his cigarettes and a flask of coffee, his patience was infinite, like that of the predators whose lives he has chronicled in decades of filming on these plains.

Suddenly the cheetahs were up and running. They had spotted a female Tommy with a fawn. In seconds they had quickened their pace, from a canter to a gallop to a blistering sprint. In vain the fawn jinked to stay in front. Tail in the air, the female cheetah reached out a forepaw and sent the young Tommy tumbling. In a flash she had it by the throat. By the time the dust had settled its life had been snuffed out among the flowers.

Above the whirr of Hugo's camera I could hear the crunch of flesh and bone as the two cheetahs fed hurriedly, bolting each mouthful lest they should be chased off their kill by marauding hyenas or surprised by the Blood Brothers, whose paths they were bound to cross sooner or later. Already a tawny eagle had drifted down to wait on the ground close by. Fifteen minutes later there was nothing left but a dark stain on the turf.

Afterwards, brother and sister sat up and faced each other like bookends, then licked each other clean and set off towards the nearest kopje, where a fig tree cast its welcoming shadow across the grass.

We, too, sought the shade and picnicked under the tree while the cats slept in the rocks. Above us an eagle owl sat among the branches, hunched like a cowled monk, waiting for darkness; and in the dust at my feet the sun glinted on a flint scraper, a Stone Age relic which showed that man, too, had lived here long ago in Africa's lost age of innocence.

The sun passed down. The cheetahs slept on. It was indescribably peaceful.

In every direction I could look out and see no sign of human presence; only a timeless world of grass and sky, larks in the wind and gazelles on the move again after the midday torpor. Zebras squealed in the cooling air, and flights of sandgrouse winged overhead from distant waterholes.

When the grass is green and the wildebeest are on the plains there is nowhere I would rather be than in the Serengeti; but soon the dry season would return and the migrating herds would leave their calving grounds to the Grant's gazelles, the kori bustards and the whirling dust devils.

For me, too, it was time to go. Other odysseys were already under way. On my journey down from the Ngorongoro Highlands I had passed clouds of white storks spiralling on the thermals as they gained height for their long flight back to Europe. At Hugo's camp, sitting one morning under a flat-topped thorn tree, I listened to the sweet and instantly familiar voice of another long-distance traveller. It was a willow warbler, linking two different worlds with its silver song; and I realised with a sudden stab of nostalgia that the next time I heard it would be among the damp springtime hazel thickets and bluebell woods of home.

Chapter Seven
In the Swamps of Bangweulu

Stealthily, and with only the stars to steer by, the canoe slid deeper into the Bangweulu swamps. Our two Zambian boatmen, muffled against the chill in old army greatcoats and balaclavas, alternatively poled and paddled us down a labyrinth of narrow channels.

When at last the bows grounded on soft mud we got out and waded knee-deep along a drowned game trail in the reeds. The clear water, so pleasant to paddle in by day, was now bone-clenchingly cold and we were glad to reach the hide. Perched on stilts atop an old termite mound, it was a flimsy thing of poles and thatch; but at least we could dry our feet and settle down with a flask of coffee to wait for sunrise.

What had lured us to these remote wetlands in north-western Zambia was the legendary sitatunga, an aquatic antelope so rare and elusive that big-game hunters will happily pay thousands of pounds to shoot one. It is a creature of extraordinary shyness. Sometimes it hides deep in the papyrus for days on end. Often it will lie submerged for hours, its lyrate horns laid back over its neck and only its muzzle above water. The sitatunga is probably the most secretive mammal in Africa, and Bangweulu the best place to see it.

Out in the darkness the swamp lay still, held in a single silence, but as the first red hint of dawn seeped over the eastern horizon, the marsh birds awoke. Senegal coucals swung on the reed stems, their black-crowned heads and cinnamon wings standing out sharply against the green walls of papyrus. Soon the entire swamp seemed to throb with their strange, bubbling cries.

The sun came up fast. Flocks of waterfowl poured overhead: knob-nosed geese, flurries of egrets, wavering streamers of sacred ibis. Drenched and glistening in the amber light, the great fen stretched to the skyline: 2,500 square miles of deltas, reeds and floating sudd.

I did not see the sitatunga appear. One moment there was nothing but an emptiness of papyrus and elephant grass. The next, a horned apparition had detached itself from the shadows, a sleek young bull, his face as barbaric as a tribal mask, his chocolate coat set off with handsome white blazes.

For fully five minutes he remained frozen, one splay-footed foreleg held off the ground in mid-stride as he sniffed the air. Then, very slowly, he lowered his head and began to feed.

Bangweulu — 'the place where the earth meets the sky' — is the deep and secret heart of Africa. It is also, fittingly perhaps, the last resting-place of the heart of David Livingstone, who died here in 1873 after seven long years looking for the source of the Nile.

On the long trip north from Lusaka to Livingstone's grave we drove for miles through shady miombo woodlands to the land of the Balala people, whose name means sleep. The Balala are a cheerful tribe. We passed their villages in the miombo* and their cassava gardens and the peeled roots of manioc — their staple diet — left in roadside streams to soak in pallid heaps like dead men's fingers.

Our destination lay down a dusty track near the Lulimala River. In the village nearby, a visitor's book was produced for us to sign in the bleak little room which serves as the local clinic.

The place where Livingstone died is marked by a simple stone memorial in a dappled glade. He had set out in 1886 to find the source of the Nile, but ended up 1,500 miles in the wrong direction, struggling through the Bangweulu swamps.

In April 1873, wracked by fever and terminally weakened by chronic dysentery, he was brought in a litter to Chief Chitambo's village, just beyond the floodplain, where he died on 1 May, kneeling in prayer at his bedside.

Afterwards his followers eviscerated his corpse and buried his heart in a metal box beneath a mupundu tree. Then the body was smeared with salt inside and out, and left like a catfish to dry in the sun. Two weeks later they wrapped his preserved cadaver in calico and carried it, trussed in a shroud of bark sewn up with sailcloth, all the way to the coast at Bagamoyo, more than 900 miles away.

Today, those who follow in Livingstone's footsteps do so in less arduous fashion with the benefit of anti-malaria tablets, four-wheel-drive vehicles and comfortable sleeping quarters. Our camp at Mandamata on the edge of the Chimbwi floodplain offered half a dozen thatched rondavels, all with mod cons, including hot showers, and an airy dining room where each day began with enormous eggs-and-bacon breakfasts.

From here we entered the surrounding seas of ripening grass, cruising by Land-Rover through archipelagos of termite mounds that rise above the flatness of the plains like the tumuli of a vanished race. Larks and plovers filled the air with plaintive cries. Reedbuck and oribi watched us pass, and large herds of tsessebe, fleetest of all the plains antelope, stared at us with long, lugubrious faces until their nerve broke and they cantered away.

Then, suddenly, no more anthills, no more trees. Only the interminable waterlands of the Chimbwi floodplain. Here, every year after the long rains, the swollen waters of Lake Bangweulu pour out of the swamps and spill across the land for nearly twenty miles. Now they had receded once more, leaving a

* Open woodlands composed mainly of broadleaved *brachystegia* and *Julbernardia* trees, covering vast expanses of southern Africa.

Top: In Tsavo national park, when the ivory poaching was at its height, dead elephants outnumbered the living. *(Jonathan Scott)*

Bottom: Black rhino: Tanzania's Ngorongoro Crater is one of the last strongholds for this highly endangered species. *(Brian Jackman)*

Top: Vultures – Africa's dark angels of death – are quick to spot kills on the Serengeti plains. *(Brian Jackman)*

Bottom: The wildebeest may look ungainly but it is the most successful antelope in Africa, evolved to survive the rigours of its migratory life-style. *(Jonathan Scott)*

Top: The Serengeti is home to all kinds of carnivores, large and small; but none so majestic as the lion. *(Jonathan Scott)*

Bottom: A golden jackal, one of the smaller denizens of Tanzania's famous Ngorongoro Crater. *(Jonathan Scott)*

Top: Serengeti sunrise; the best time to be out on the plains if you want to watch lions hunting. *(Brian Jackman)*

Bottom: Every year the Serengeti wildebeest gather on the short grass plains where the calves are born in February. *(Jonathan Scott)*

green flush of grass for huge herds of black lechwe, an antelope found nowhere else in Africa.

In places the retreating floods still lay in sun-warmed shallows where we paddled ankle-deep among congregations of birds in numbers beyond counting: wattled cranes and saddlebill storks, lumbering fleets of pelicans and swift squadrons of pratincoles. Sometimes a distant flock would erupt into the blue, disturbed, perhaps, by the sudden appearance of an African marsh harrier sailing over the reed-beds.

And finally, the great swamp itself, with its dawn mists and drenching dews, its lily ponds and Batwa fishing villages marooned deep in the papyrus. Here, punting down Bangweulu's pellucid channels, we came across another mysterious spirit of the swamps — the ghostly grey shoebill stork — and listened to the cry of the fish eagle whose yelping voice sounded to Livingstone as if it were 'calling to someone in the other world'.

No wonder that even Livingstone, fatally ill as he was, should have been moved by the magic of the swamps. 'Men were hunting,' he wrote in his journal in late March 1873, 'and we passed near large herds of antelope which made a rushing, plunging noise as they ran and sprang among the waters. A lion had wandered into this world of water and anthills and roared night and morning.'

Today, more than a century later, Livingstone's world is still a pristine wilderness. The antelope still run and the Marsh lions still roar. Whatever happens elsewhere in Africa, one feels that Bangweulu's immense horizons and huge marshland skies will be just the same a hundred years from now.

From Lake Bangweulu I wanted to continue to the Luangwa Valley, the home of Zambia's finest national park, which lies some 160 miles to the south-east. By road this would have entailed an arduous cross-country trek over the Muchinga Escarpment, whose steep slopes rise for more than 2,000 feet above the western borders of the park. Luckily a light aircraft had been laid on to complete this leg of the safari.

The plane had managed to land on a makeshift strip at the edge of the floodplain without getting bogged down in the mud, but could not fly back to the Luangwa without refuelling. A drum of Avgas was brought out from the camp at Mandamata, but of course there was no pump in the middle of the bush. So, as is often the way in Africa, the pilot had to improvise by sucking at one end of the fuel pipe until the Avgas began to flow, after which he could fill up his empty tanks. Unfortunately he sucked too hard and swallowed a mouthful of fuel.

Somehow, coughing and spluttering, he managed to complete the refuelling and waved us aboard. 'Hurry,' he croaked, his face still red and his eyes streaming, 'I'll feel better at altitude.' I hoped he would. With his desperate expression and his shirt reeking of spilled fuel, he did not exactly inspire confidence among his passengers. Nor was their anxiety set at rest when, after finally becoming airborne, he suddenly fumbled for the window and retched violently into the slipstream.

He mopped his brow with a large handkerchief. 'Phew,' he gasped. 'I feel much better now. Gentlemen, you may now smoke if you wish.' Not surprisingly, no one took him up on this suggestion.

Eventually, to everyone's relief, we landed safely in the Luangwa, but our adventures were not yet over. Waiting on the airstrip for a vehicle to come out from the lodge and pick us up, we unloaded our bags and stood chatting on the strip in the strong wind. 'I'll keep the engine running,' said the pilot. 'It's not worth switching off as I'll be taking off again in a few moments.'

Unfortunately he had forgotten to place chocks under the wheels, and now, in the strong wind, with the propeller still turning, the aircraft had begun to roll away down the strip. He must have seen the startled look on my face, for he spun round. 'Oh my God, my plane,' he cried, and set off in hot pursuit. Somehow he managed to wrench open a door and fling himself inside, his legs trailing in the dust as he yanked at the brake and finally brought the plane to rest.

Later, back at the lodge with a much-needed drink, somebody told me that his exploits were well-known in Zambia. It was even suggested that he was worthy of a mention in the *Guinness Book of Records* as the pilot who had successfully survived the greatest number of crashes.

July in Zambia is winter's end: cold dawns, golden days, the sky an impeccable eggshell blue. Soon the air will fill with dust and the smoke of grass fires, but as yet the immense horizons remain clear and sharp-etched.

Down in the South Luangwa Valley the land is drying fast. Already the buffalo have left the hills, moving down from the Muchinga Escarpment to converge on the river. Crouched in the tall *kasensi* grass, the Luangwa prides await their coming. From now until the rains break in November, eight out of every ten lion kills in the valley will be buffalo.

South Luangwa is Zambia's finest national park. Here, less than ninety minutes by air from Lusaka, you step out into the crackling dry heat to be whisked by open-topped Land-Rover into a world as remote from the twentieth century as anywhere you could hope to find even in this ancient continent.

It is the kind of place which, normally, if one had stumbled across it by accident, would have remained a jealously guarded secret. But nowadays even paradise must pay its way. Zambia needs the hard cash which tourism provides, and which is the most persuasive reason for preserving the game. That is why I have no guilty feelings about urging anyone to visit South Luangwa and swell the ranks of those who, like me, believe it to be one of the hallowed places of the earth.

Imagine a wilderness the size of Devon. Enclose it with great blowsy trees — figs and tamarinds, 1,000-year-old baobabs, stag-headed leadwoods, lofty glades of proud old winterthorns and endless aisles of cathedral mopane. Ignore the steeple-sized anthills and the result is not unlike a neglected English country park, complete with flaring autumn colours.

Add a mighty river as wide as the Thames. Add more water in the distinctive shapes of oxbow lagoons known locally as *dambos*, each one a ghost of the river's former meanderings, shaded by cool ebony groves, carpeted with Nile cabbage, seething with frogs, fish and herons.

Now bring it all to life. For every mile of river add at least thirty hippos; for every sandbank, a score of crocodiles. Populate the plains and thickets with the fleeting shapes of elands and kudu. Fill the shadows with lions and leopards then, to complete the scene, bring in a herd of elephants marching down to drink.

The only people in the valley are the few visitors lucky enough to stay at one of the half-dozen comfortable and unobtrusive safari lodges. Unlike in East Africa, where tourist vehicles sometimes outnumber the vultures around a kill, you seldom see another soul.

The distances are so great, the bush so dense. Within minutes the trees close around you like a tide, surrounding you with soft-calling doves and the echoing depths of the mopane — magical woodlands whose leaves fold together in the heat of the day like sleeping butterflies, reducing transpiration, letting in the light.

Game-viewing by Land-Rover has its advantages. One day, driving through the park in mid-afternoon, we surprised a leopard at the very moment it had grabbed an impala. As soon as it saw us it dragged its victim into a *donga*, where it crouched between the narrow banks, pale eyes fixing us as it proceeded to throttle the still-struggling antelope.

Suddenly, the leopard began to lash its tail. Its haunches quivered. Then it was charging straight at us, tail up, and at that very moment the driver stalled the vehicle.

There was no time to be afraid. I simply froze, unable to comprehend what my eyes were telling me, that the leopard was coming for us. But at the last moment its nerve broke. There was a yellow blur as it swerved around us and streaked away — beautiful to behold in its fluid, bounding grace — to disappear into a dense stand of reeds.

These sudden glimpses of heart-pounding savagery, while providing the high points of many a campfire yarn, are nevertheless rare interludes, ripples of violence which only briefly disturb the valley's languid calm. Mostly it is a benign and drowsy place, lulled by the hypnotic calls of black-collared barbets, the sombre voice of ground hornbills and the whine of cicadas. Often in the Luangwa I awoke to the thrilling sound of lions roaring. But at the end of it all what I remember with the greatest pleasure are the gentle voices of the sweet-throated turtle doves and the sad refrain of water dikkops falling over Mfuwe Lagoon.

The ultimate experience in the Luangwa is to explore it on foot. It was here that Norman Carr, former warden and now the valley's grand old statesman, pioneered walking safaris in the 1960s. He it was who gave me my baptism in bush-bashing here in 1978; and if walking in the tall 'adrenalin grass' tends to raise your levels of apprehension, there is always the comforting presence of your *fundi*, the professional game scout in whose footsteps you follow, and whose heavy-calibre elephant gun is ready as a last resort.

Norman Carr was born in Mozambique. He was sent to England to be educated but at the age of nineteen returned to Africa where he has lived ever since — except for five years' active service in the Second World War, which he finished as an infantry battalion captain. In his twenties he became a freelance ivory hunter in what was then Portuguese East Africa, but later underwent the classic conversion from poacher to gamekeeper, first as an elephant control officer and ultimately as Chief Game Warden in the Northern Rhodesian Game Department — a job he held until he was flattened by a buffalo while tracking elephant in tall grass. Fortunately he survived and after a spell in hospital he returned to the bush to open up the Kafue National Park.

During his stay in Kafue he adopted two lion cubs, Big Boy and Little Boy, which he successfully raised and returned to the wild, as George Adamson was to do in northern Kenya. Later, he retired from the Game Department and moved into the Luangwa Valley to set up the safari business which has brought him friends from all over the world and established the South Luangwa National Park as one of Africa's finest animal sanctuaries.

It was with Norman that I first learned how to meet Africa on level terms, with my feet on the ground. Only then did I realise how much I had missed when sitting in a vehicle. Only on foot would I have seen the rare Pel's fishing owl — a denizen of the ebony groves with a cry which has been likened to that of a lost soul falling into a bottomless pit. Only on foot would I have caught the mingled scents of dust and hot grass, wild African lavender and elephant dung.

On a return visit in 1982 my guide was Robin Pope, one of Norman Carr's protégés. Quiet and bespectacled, he has the looks of a poet but is as tough as old biltong. Then only thirty-one, he was already a bush veteran with his own idyllic small camp at Nsefu on a bend of the Luangwa River.

It was Robin who showed me a 2,000-strong breeding colony of yellow-billed storks at Chipela Lagoon; who conjured up four black rhinos in one afternoon and who found the legendary fishing owl. It was Robin who first taught me to recognise lion and leopard tracks, who pointed out ant-bear holes and wild bees' nests, picked sprigs of wild jasmine to sniff as we walked, and put a name to every bird call. And it was Robin who quietly shepherded us to safety when two elephants began to demonstrate, spreading their ears and searching for our scent with curling trunks.

Of all big game it is the elephant which commands the greatest respect. In the Luangwa their dung was everywhere; so were their footprints, holes the size of dustbin lids pile-driven into the muddy beds of dried-up *dambos*. Sometimes we would see them standing as if becalmed, far out in oceans of bleached blond grass, motionless except for the idle flapping of huge ears. Or we would watch a solitary bull drifting with a silence uncanny for so great a beast, a grey ghost melting like smoke between the trees.

At such times I could not help recalling the words of the American writer, Henry Beston, engraved in stone beneath the statue of a lechwe antelope at Lusaka Airport: 'In a world older and more complete than ours they move finished and complete, gifted with extensions of the senses we have lost or never attained, living by voices we shall never hear.'

Sadly, every Eden has its serpent and the Luangwa is no exception. When I first visited the valley it was said to hold 100,000 elephants and perhaps 4,000 black rhinos. For both species it was an unrivalled stronghold. Since then, commercial poaching spreading south like an infection from Kenya and Tanzania has finished the rhino and left only a fragment of its great elephant herds. Even now, despite the international ban on ivory trading, corruption at every level ensures that elephants continue to die for the price of their tusks, leaving both Zambia and its finest national park increasingly impoverished. In 1983 there were still maybe 1,000 rhinos hidden in the valley, but they were going fast. That year, early one morning at Chinzombo Lodge, a fusillade of shots rang out from across the river. Hurriedly an anti-poaching patrol was assembled and Phil Berry, its commander, invited me to tag along.

There followed a mad, helter-skelter ride along dirt roads. Then we left the vehicles and plunged into the mopane woodlands on foot. There were a dozen of us, all in jungle-green bush fatigues, and everyone except me carrying a rifle.

Phil Berry set a cracking pace. In the gasping heat my shirt was soon soaked with sweat. Thorns tore at our arms and legs, and tsetse flies added to our torment.

In a little while we saw vultures circling above the trees, but to our surprise, when we crept forward to investigate we found the body of a fourteen-foot-long python. The snake had been killed by a single bite to the throat, and was clearly not the work of the rhino poachers so we hurried on.

Once, from the shadows of a dense thicket, there came a sudden terrifying snort. '*Chipembere*,' whispered a tracker. Rhino! Hastily we each chose a tree and dived behind it in case the ungrateful animal decided to charge his protectors; but in the end it lumbered away.

At the end of four hours we had nothing to show for our efforts except a strip of red rag tied to a bush in our path.'Probably a warning left by the gang,' said Phil Berry. 'It means stop or we'll shoot, or something like that.'

I was exhausted; but for Phil and his rangers this was all in a day's work; part of the never-ending bush war being waged against the poachers. Sadly, despite all their efforts, the park proved too big to patrol effectively with the meagre resources available. The corruption went too deep, the temptations were too great and the poachers too numerous. No matter how many were caught, more kept on coming until the last rhino had fallen.

The Luangwa rhinos will never return, but elephants are still common around the lodges and at least the scale of poaching has greatly diminished since the ivory trade ban, giving hope that the herds may yet recover. Mercifully, too, the rest of the game is still abundant, and leopards seem more numerous than ever.

Chapter Eight
Night Watch

Daylight hours in the Luangwa Valley are filled with constant life and movement — lions mating, kudu browsing, a Thornicroft's giraffe (a species unique to the valley) reaching up to pluck the sausage-shaped fruit from a kigelia tree. From the drowsy woodlands comes the cackle of red-billed wood hoopoes. Pied kingfishers hover over the Luangwa River and, high above, bateleur eagles rock in the thermals on black and white wings. Out in midstream, pods of hippos lie half-submerged, luxuriating in the muddy waters. All day they doze, moving only to lift their heads in a cavernous yawn, to bellow and snort and then subside again, leaving nothing but their nostrils and frog-like eyes above the surface.

The river is the Luangwa's lifeblood. Coiling and uncoiling on its way down the 450-mile valley to join the Zambezi, it dominates the park throughout the year. The valley is older than East Africa's Great Rift, and so wide that only on the clearest days can you see the Muchinga Escarpment which marks its western limits. But nothing could live here without the river.

In the wet season it bursts its banks, replenishing the grassy *dambos* and oxbows, creating lagoons where elephants come to wallow. Even in the dry season, when the air quivers at furnace heat, when the Christmas beetles shrill from the rain trees and the Luangwa shrinks to a torpid trickle, the animals never go thirsty.

At Chibembe lodge, sitting with a cold beer under the shade of the tall, evergreen *Trichelia emetica* trees, I found it a constant delight to watch the comings and goings of animals on the opposite bank through the long, hot Zambian day. Then, in late afternoon, the sun seems suddenly to lose its heat. Shadows lengthen and a male bushbuck, coming down warily to drink, churns up a patch of mud with his horns. Not far away, hiding in the deep shade of an ebony grove, a fishing owl sits, waiting for the sun to vanish behind the Muchinga Escarpment.

Now the light is going fast, and for half an hour there is an increased burst of activity along the river's crumbling banks before the night watch takes over. Egyptian geese fly past in pairs, calling noisily as they alight on a sandbar where the river bends. On the opposite bank two elephants emerge from the trees and shuffle cautiously down a hippo trail. With trunks extended to check their way, they go to drink. Later, maybe, they will leave the park and cross the river on a crop-raiding spree among the nearby villages, hurrying back to safety just as dawn is breaking.

High up in the crown of a sausage tree sits a pearl-spotted owlet. Its bright yellow eyes stare down through the leaves. The river mirrors the sun's red afterglow, throwing into sharp silhouette the flitting shapes of a few late white-rumped swifts as they hawk for insects. The swifts are joined by a handful of bats, which as the sky darkens become more numerous and swarm out over the water. Upstream and downstream, the riverbanks echo to the bellows of hippos, intermittently drowning out the anguished cries of water dikkops. The last doves fall silent, and in the stillness the night-long rasping of the cicadas begins.

Now is the time to put on warmer clothes and climb into the open back of a stripped-down Land-Cruiser. Night drives, with an armed guard and a powerful hand-held spotlight plugged into the dashboard, reveal a secret world that is hidden by day.

Hippos emerge from the river at dusk to graze and are scattered about in the undergrowth. Caught in the spotlight, they are purplish-brown on top and a dusty scalded pink underneath.

Bumping along the rutted trail it is sometimes hard to follow the spotlight's beam. Swiftly it flicks from tree to tree, scything across the tops of anthills, cutting a path through the long grass, washing everything it touches in the yellow glow of tungsten.

We turn off the track, approach an oxbow lagoon and, cutting the engine, roll slowly to a halt. After the rains this lagoon was full. Now it has shrunk to a moon-shaped curve of shallow water set in a bowl of dried ruts and wallows. Small bats, their creamy-brown bellies flashing, spin and tumble through the light as they hunt over the lagoon. Beneath them, pairs of dull red lights — the eyes of crocodiles — move with sinister purpose across the surface. In front of each pair, shoals of fish set the water boiling as they scatter to escape.

We start up and head back to the track, passing through the film of dust we raised on our way to the lagoon five minutes before. As the spotlight resumes its sweeping rhythms it picks up more lights twinkling and shining in clusters all about us, like distant harbours viewed from a ship at sea. These scattered constellations are groups of antelope — puku, impala and sometimes waterbuck — standing tense and ready to run.

Moments later we stop again, this time for two small lights low down in the grass. By looking through binoculars along the line of the beam I can just make out a pair of dark ears. The ears move forward, and a genet treads slowly through the pool of light, its spotted coat of moonlight grey and long, boldly striped tail perfectly camouflaged among the shadows of the tangled stems. Then it bounds off with a rippling gait into the surrounding darkness.

Changes in habitat as we follow the track are marked by accompanying smells and subtle temperature changes in the night air; a sudden coolness on the face as we pass through an ebony grove; then back into the dusty warmth of grassland studded with combretum thickets and down to the river through the musty sweet odour of fresh elephant dung.

Travelling parallel to the river, we move a little faster, not stopping for impala, bushbuck or puku. Only the more elusive animals will detain us now. But moments later two bright points of light high up in a tree bring us skidding to a halt with a whispered cry of 'Eyes!' I wonder if it is a leopard, but it turns out to be a bushbaby. When it turns its head directly into the beam, the reflection from its eyes is as bright as sunlight on polished brass.

Suddenly, as we pass through a patch of woodland, a branch cracks like a gunshot. Even without the spotlight there is no mistaking the huge silhouette which emerges on to the path ahead, or the pale gleam of curving tusks. Other elephants are crashing among the trees to our left, while from the other side comes a strident trumpet blast. In the darkness they are all around us, and I notice our game guard prudently sliding a bullet into his .458 Parker–Hale elephant gun. But the herd melts away as swiftly as it materialised, leaving only a strong whiff of dung in the damp air.

As we drive on through the park every moving gleam in the grass brings a vision of a predator — leopard, hyena, wild dog or lion. In the Luangwa, all are possible. We drive on, heading back to camp across an open stretch of termitaria grassland, where anthill mounds cast lunar shadows. Some are less than three feet high. Others are rambling cones crowned with scrub, or lofty pyramids which appear to be swallowing up whole tamarind trees.

From behind one such mound an aardvark emerges, recalling for me the immortal description by Alan Root, the wildlife film-maker: The aardvark; first word in the dictionary — last word in anteater design.

We are lucky. This animal is seldom seen. Even our driver is excited. It is a curious creature. The hair on its flanks and shoulders is thin, on the legs dense. Rather than turning and galloping off, it simply pivots on its tail and trots slowly away, ears laid back tight along its body as it weaves through the undergrowth.

A short while later we spot a porcupine, another secretive animal, a shivering fan of quills bobbing away into the night. And then, at last, what we have all been hoping for: a cluster of eyes in the grass that reveals itself as a whole pride of lions. There are nine altogether, all of them females. Sinuously they rub against each other, licking and softly moaning in the prelude to the hunt which is about to begin. I can see from the thin line of their bellies that they have not eaten.

Then suddenly they are off, fanning out through the grass at a steady walk with us trailing behind. Out of the darkness comes the gasping bark of alarmed impala. Caught in the beam, their eyes glow like emeralds. Soon afterwards a volley of growls tells us that we have missed the kill, and almost at once, out of nowhere, two splendid male lions come trotting over the road in front of us, heavy manes swinging as they hurry to join the feast.

The pride have killed on the far side of a *dambo* which is difficult to cross in the dark. Besides, we have been out for two hours and supper will be ready back at the lodge. We leave the night to the lions and turn for home. Nightjars fly up from the dust in front of us, flickering through the beams of our headlights as we hurry back, and even as the lamps of Chibembe begin to shine through the trees, a side-striped jackal goes loping past to disappear down a narrow *donga*. This time, unusually for the Luangwa, we have failed to find a leopard; but it would be churlish to complain. Besides, I knew there would be other parks, other game drives to find the cat that walks by itself.

Chapter Nine
Across the Wide Zambezi

Suspended in space, 300 feet above the Zambezi Gorge in the strange no-man's land beyond the Zambian border post, I could see the spray clouds rising from the mile-long rim of the Victoria Falls, and hear the thunder of the falling foam.

As a curtain-raiser to Zimbabwe there is no finer or more dramatic introduction than this; to enter the country on foot, crossing from the Mosi-oa-Tunya Hotel on the Zambian side by way of the Falls Bridge with its dizzy views into the abyss beneath and historic memories of secret meetings conducted in closed railway carriages to determine the future of the land once called Rhodesia.

A lot of water has flowed under the bridge since then. Today Zimbabwe has put the bitterness of war behind her and opened her doors and her heart to tourism. At the Victoria Falls Hotel — surely the grandest hotel in all Africa — guests sip Malawi shandies on the terrace to the music of a Marimba band, waiting for the smell of barbecued steaks to call them to supper under the stars.

The falls themselves are only a few minutes' walk from the hotel and lie just inside the Victoria Falls National Park. During March and April more than 100 million gallons of water per minute race over the black basalt lips of the precipice to plunge into the gorge over 300 feet below. But at any time of the year, even in November when the Zambezi is at its lowest, it is a stupendous place.

Above the falls, rainbows hang in the drifting spray which gave rise to its local name of Mosi-oa-Tunya — 'the Smoke that Thunders'. Its constant drenchings have created what is in effect a local rainforest, where maidenhair ferns grow in the shade and trumpeter hornbills — large black-and-white birds with braying voices — fly through the mist above the crashing waters.

Very different is Hwange National Park, Zimbabwe's greatest wildlife stronghold. In Hwange there is no permanent water. Only the pans — shallow pools sustained by ramshackle pumping stations — keep the game alive through the dry season. Often, driving through the sunstruck thorns in the breathless mid-morning heat, I would long to feel again the cool moisture of the falls on my skin; yet there was no denying the magic of this hot, flat land. In Hwange the world is still a clean and billowy place; 5,500 square miles of soft Kalahari sand overlaid with wide grassy *vleis*, shady teak forests and glades of ancient camelthorns.

The majority of visitors seemed content to watch the animals from the manicured lawns of Hwange's elegant safari lodge, to the soothing clink of iced drinks. Black-collared barbets fluted their monotonous duets from the treetops as a constant procession of kudu and zebras came trooping in to the waterhole. It was all very peaceful; but I had chosen to stay in the more secluded surroundings of Dave Rushworth's bush camp.

Rushworth, a sandy-haired bush veteran, at once demonstrated his camping skills by cooking a delicious supper of steaks and *burrewurst* which he grilled on the embers and then steeped in a rich alcoholic sauce of wine, onions, beer and tomatoes. Afterwards, cupping our hands to the fire as the temperature plummeted towards zero, we sat and talked while hyenas whooped in the distant darkness.

Next morning at dawn, having slept the night in a tree-house perched twenty feet above the ground, I drove with Rushworth to a nearby hide overlooking a *vlei* and waited for the game to emerge. It was July — the African winter — and so sharp was the air, so cold and silent that when a bull eland emerged some 300 yards away I could hear the click of the tendons in its forelegs. He approached slowly, head nodding in time with his steady gait, and at each nod the sun caught the points of his horns and made them shine like Zulu spears.

Elsewhere in Zimbabwe the animals seemed shyer. At Mana Pools, a beautiful national park on the banks of the Zambezi, I went for a walk with Dick Pitman, a writer who left Britain in 1979 to work for Zimbabwe's National Parks Service. Away from the river much of the park is covered with dense jesse bush and infested with tsetse flies. But along the banks, under the airy glades of giant winterthorns, you can see much farther and walking is safer.

Neither of us was armed. Besides, Pitman knew the country well. It therefore came as something of a shock when two full-grown male lions rose from a patch of long grass only a few steps in front of us. The nearest tree was much too far to reach; and in any case, to run from a lion is to invite trouble. We froze, but almost in the same instant the pair of them whirled and bolted across the Sapi sand river, while we in turn hurriedly retraced our steps and returned to camp.

Wherever I went in Zimbabwe, each game park had its resident devotee. In Hwange it had been Dave Rushworth. At Mana Pools it was John Stevens, who was then managing the newly-opened Chikwenya safari camp on the banks of the Zambezi.

In a country renowned for the excellence of its professional safari guides, John Stevens is second to none. He can read spoor as expertly as any African tracker and can call a lion out of the thornbush by bleating like an animal in distress. Like many guides he began his career as an eighteen-year-old cadet ranger with the Zimbabwe National Parks Service. 'That's where I learned how to hunt, patrol, build roads, manage a camp, capture and translocate wild animals, all those things,' he told me.

In 1982 he left the Parks Service and has been running his own safaris ever since, specialising in small groups with a strong emphasis on walking. He still loves Mana Pools, even though its once prolific black rhinos are all gone — shot by poaching gangs from Zambia, on the other side of the Zambezi.

'In 1991 we found forty-five rhinos,' he said. 'In 1992 they were down to twenty-five. In 1993 we found just six, and this year there were none. It's very sad and it makes me very angry to see what the poachers have done to this country. But at least the rest of the game is in great shape.'

Nowadays he has a new camp in the Matusadona National Park. 'Real wilderness,' he calls it. 'No tracks. We just walk. It's for people who like remote places and want to experience what it's like to track a buffalo bull for a couple of hours.'

In the bush he always carries a rifle; but in all the years he has been taking clients on safari he has had to use it only twice in self-defence. 'Once I had to shoot an elephant,' he said. 'I'd fired a warning shot but still it kept coming. In the end there was no alternative. I fired again and it dropped about six feet in front of me.'

John Stevens is not a man who is given to bravado; and when he tells you there is no time to be afraid, you believe him. 'When it's happening I'm always confident and in control,' he said. 'But afterwards, after I'd dropped the elephant, I put out my arm to show my clients how it was shaking. I wanted to let them know that even professional guides are human.'

After John Stevens had left Chikwenya the camp was later taken over by the redoubtable Jeff Stuchbury. But when I met Stuchbury he was still running the luxurious Bumi Hills Lodge, overlooking Lake Kariba.

Jeff belonged to that dwindling breed of legendary adventurers who have almost vanished elsewhere in the world, but who can still be found in the remoter corners of Africa. He was born in Southampton in 1926, but had spent most of his life in the African bush. In his time he had been a mounted policeman, tried his hand at tobacco farming and sailed around Lake Malawi as a professional crocodile hunter.

When the Zambezi Valley was flooded to create Lake Kariba, Stuchbury instantly became involved with 'Operation Noah', rescuing leopards and other animals which had become stranded by the rising waters.

With his silver beard and sunburnt hide, he looked like a younger version of George Adamson, and he shared Adamson's love of wild places. Although he was running Bumi Hills, his heart was across the water on the lonely shores of the Matusadona, where he and Veronica, his wife, kept their 'Water Wilderness' — a flotilla of houseboats moored among the reeds and lily pads of the Ume River.

Here, spirited by outboard motor into a lost world of secret creeks and winding channels, I stayed for three nights, sleeping comfortably in what looked like a floating potting shed, dining on steaks and splendid salads while time ceased and life took on a strange, dreamlike quality. I remember the fish eagles, white heads flung back as they cried from the skeletal superstructure of forests drowned when the lake was born, and the elephants that came in the dawn, grey shadows slipping through the waterside meadows of sweet panicum grass.

All day long the hippos chuckled in the sudsy carpets of Nile cabbage. Black crakes skulked in the reeds. Dragonflies glittered. Frogs gulped as if too sleepy to croak; and towards dusk, long flights of open-billed storks came pouring through the blood-red Kariba evenings as the dead trees turned black against the fading light.

Sometimes we would set out by canoe, soundlessly drifting to within a few yards of some towering tusker who would flap his huge ears at our effrontery before crashing off into the bush. Or we would paddle out at night by torchlight, shining the beam beneath our bows to watch tigerfish cruising in the weed-hung channels, while Stuchbury looked for the ruby eyes of crocodiles. One of his favourite tricks was to grab a small croc by the throat and lift it from the water. 'Cute little fellows, aren't they?' he said, as it writhed and complained in a curious, croaking voice.

Another time, Stuchbury shouldered his rifle and led me deep into the jesse bush, following paths which the Matusadona rhinos had tunnelled through the unforgiving thorns. At one point we came across a rhino midden. The dung was so fresh it was still steaming. Stuchbury was overjoyed at the thought of showing me the rhino, which could not have been far away. I muttered something which I hoped would pass for enthusiasm while surreptitiously looking round for a tree I could climb, or even an anthill to hide behind should the need arise; but fortunately the rhino chose not to show itself.

Later, when we finally emerged in more open country and my pulse had returned to normal, I began to appreciate the wild beauty of the Matusadona. There was a grassy valley, the gleam of water running brightly over coarse gravel, then a chain of deep pools under low red cliffs overhung with fig and mahogany trees; and everywhere the prints of animals, the rich, dark brown smells of elephant and buffalo. Kudu and bushbuck fled before us. Overhead a martial eagle circled slowly as the sun rose higher, and doves droned in the forest.

Back on board the houseboat, I showered while the sunset flared and faded. Later there was a fire of mopane logs in an iron brazier at the stern. Beer in hand, I sat and listened to the jangling lullaby of crickets and reed frogs, the bark of an impala on the shore. Stuchbury breathed a deep, contented sigh.

'There's nowhere quite like this, is there?' he said, and fell silent again.

In the morning I was moving on, heading down towards Gonarezhou National Park on the Mozambique border. Gonarezhou was bandit country, infiltrated by wild-eyed gangs of Renamo guerrillas bent on poaching Zimbabwe's elephants, whose ivory paid for guns from South Africa. But for the moment all thought of conflict seemed far away. Fireflies winked across the water. High above shone the Southern Cross. And all around us, eternal Africa, and a peace of mind beyond price.

I did not know it then, but this was the last I would see of this remarkable man. Tragically, Jeff Stuchbury died of cancer in 1992, aged sixty-five, depriving Zimbabwe of one of its most highly respected men of the wild.

Chapter Ten
Horn of the Elephant

The Super Cub bucked viciously in the hot African sky. To the east I could see the immense horizons of Mozambique. To the south lay South Africa's great Kruger National Park. But our concentration was centred on the ground 500 feet below, where our shadow flitted over the treetops of Gonarezhou, the wildest national park in Zimbabwe. Somewhere down there, hidden among the baobabs and endless mopane glades, was an elephant called Kabakwe, and our intention was to find him.

Gonarezhou means 'Horn of the Elephant' in the Shangaan language — a fitting name for the home of Zimbabwe's most famous tusker. In a country of big elephants, Gonarezhou has always been renowned for its giant bulls, and the veteran Kabakwe was the king of them all. Although he must have roamed the low veld for at least half a century, his existence was not confirmed until 1979, just four years before my visit.

About that time, stories of an old bull with colossal tusks had begun to circulate among the local Shangaan tribesmen. It was they who called him Kabakwe — 'the Big One'. Then he was seen and photographed for the first time, and almost overnight he became a living legend, a walking national monument.

It was not just his bulk that distinguished him. Even in Gonarezhou there were bigger bulls than the five-ton Kabakwe. What made him unique were his tusks; six-foot scimitars of dull yellow ivory, thick as telegraph poles and so perfectly matched that even then, before the poaching holocaust of the 1980s sent prices soaring, they could easily have fetched £20,000. An elephant's tusks are its upper incisors, which continue to grow throughout its life; and at 120 pounds apiece, Kabakwe's must have been two of the heaviest teeth on earth, exceeded at that time perhaps only by those of Mafunyane, his South African rival in the Kruger.

Their quality, too, was outstanding. Many elephants damage their tusks. Often they have a 'working' tusk, which they favour when feeding or digging for water, and which will wear down at a faster rate. But Kabakwe's tusks were not only exceptionally large; they were smooth, symmetrical and in perfect condition.

It was said of the Gonarezhou elephants that they had the longest tusks and the shortest tempers in Africa. Certainly there is a history of huge tuskers in the region going back to the days of the old-time ivory hunters, when this meeting-place of three countries — Rhodesia (as it then was), Mozambique

Top: Even at rest, cheetahs keep a low profile. They have many potential enemies; not only lions and hyenas but even other cheetahs. *(Jonathan Scott)*

Bottom: First light in the Serengeti; to follow the animals across the plains makes for an unrivalled sense of freedom. *(Jonathan Scott)*

Top: Saddlebilled stork. The name refers to the yellow 'saddle' on its slightly upturned black and red beak.
(Jonathan Scott)

Bottom: Male waterbuck; one of the heaviest African antelopes, easily recognised by its beautiful U-shaped horns.
(David Coulson)

Above: Anti-poaching patrol in the Luangwa Valley. Sadly, despite their efforts, the fight to save Zambia's black rhinos was lost. *(Brian Jackman)*

Left: The author in Zambia's Luangwa Valley, one of the best places in Africa for walking safaris. *(Brian Jackman)*

Top: Cape buffalo bull. The heavy horns are formidable weapons, yet many buffalo are pulled down by lions.
(David Coulson)

Bottom: Lilac-breasted rollers. This gorgeous bird gets its name from its spectacular somersaulting display flight.
(Jonathan Scott)

and South Africa — was known as Crooks' Corner; a lawless land beyond the pale, where poachers could cross borders with impunity. One of the most famous ivory hunters who hung out here in the 1920s was Cecil Barnard, who earned considerable notoriety for shooting another legendary bull called Dhulalamithi ('Taller-than-Trees'). For twenty-eight years Barnard pursued an even bigger bull called Isilwane across the low veld; but when at last he had him in his sights he could not bear to pull the trigger. From that day on, his grandson Willem told me, the veteran hunter put aside his gun and became one of the founding fathers of the Kruger National Park.

Since then, further disturbances in the form of anti-tsetse operations, regular incursions by Renamo guerrillas from Mozambique and a disturbing upsurge in poaching had done little to soothe the extreme edginess of the park's 6,000 elephants. Many were blown up by landmines laid along the Mozambique border during Zimbabwe's bloody war of independence. Others, including Kabakwe himself, had lost the tips of their trunks, agonisingly severed by poachers' snares.

Only the week before I arrived, a gang armed with automatic assault rifles had moved in from Mozambique and gunned down an entire group of fourteen elephants. That was why Kabakwe now wore a radio collar. Sedated with the aid of a tranquillising dart, he had been fitted with a transmitter so that even in the thickest bush the park rangers could keep track of him by tuning in to his signals.

But now, as we swooped low over the treetops, there were no signals to guide us. The batteries had packed up and for several weeks nothing had been seen or heard of Kabakwe until the previous day when, by a stroke of luck, Denis Van Eyssen, the park's senior ranger, had spotted him from the air on a routine patrol.

Below us, vultures came boiling up from the body of a kudu caught in a poacher's snare, and we slid away to avoid them. As we resumed our course, Van Eyssen suddenly jabbed a finger at the scrub to our right. 'Kabakwe,' he shouted above the engine's roar.

And there he was, together with two askaris, or young guard bulls, instantly recognisable by his radio collar and massive tusks. There was a dull gleam of ivory as he whirled about, ears flapping in alarm as we roared directly overhead. Then all three animals put up their tails and ran for the trees.

Back at the park headquarters we set out again, this time by Land-Rover, bumping down the dusty game trails to the spot where we had seen him melting away into the mopane woodlands.

From here it had to be on foot, following Van Eyssen as he cast around for Kabakwe's spoor. In one hand he carried a .458 elephant gun; in the other a small muslin bag filled with wood ash. From time to time he gently shook the bag and watched intently as each puff of ash drifted away on the warm air. 'I hope the wind stays in our favour,' he whispered. 'Because I'd much rather shoot you than have to kill Kabakwe.'

We found him half a mile from the spot where we had left the Land-Rover, feeding placidly with his two companions. Again Van Eyssen flicked the ash bag. The wind was still carrying our scent away from the elephants. We crept closer. Only thirty yards now. Surely he could see us? He was standing broadside on, idly plucking leaves from the coppiced mopane. Then, slowly, he turned to face us, four square and formidable, yet still mercifully oblivious to our presence.

I was aware of a sudden dryness in my throat, and I hoped I could hold my camera steady. Kabakwe had been photographed before, but never from the front and certainly never as close as this.

Afterwards, driving back through the deepening light of late afternoon with the Chilojo cliffs glowing red and a Verreaux's eagle sailing over the golden woodlands, the image of Kabakwe burned in my mind. The two young bulls had been uneasy. Perhaps sensing our presence, they had sought our scent with upraised trunks as we crouched in the scrub; but Kabakwe had remained unperturbed. Even now I could see the wise-seeming eyes set in the great wrinkled head; the shrunken temples that spoke his age; the huge ears, slowly swinging in the heat; and above all, the glorious sweep of those magnificent tusks. 'Man,' sighed Van Eyssen with his clipped Southern African accent, 'I've seen some tuskers in my time; but after Kabakwe the rest are just warthogs.'

Afterwards, when I had returned to England, Kabakwe's photograph duly appeared in *The Sunday Times* under a story headed 'King of the Ivories'. But there is a sad ending to this tale. In 1989, while investigating a story about ivory poaching in southern Africa, I was told that Kabakwe had been shot, and that ironically his killer was a Bulawayo dentist. Where those mighty tusks are now is anyone's guess.

Under a lofty knobthorn acacia on the edge of Hwange National Park, a lone bull elephant is resting. Ten years have passed since I was last in Zimbabwe on the trail of Kabakwe, and it feels good to be back among the golden woodlands and dry yellow grasslands of this wonderful land.

The dappled light gleams on the bull's heavy tusks. He must be well into his prime, a six-ton juggernaut, standing ten feet tall. 'Come on, old fellow,' says Alan Elliott, sitting at the wheel of our open Toyota Land-Cruiser. 'Come and say hello.'

Alan's voice is soft, his movements unhurried. In his hands he holds out a couple of acacia seedpods, soft and grey as rabbits' ears. He shakes them gently, causing the seeds inside to rattle. And suddenly the big tusker is striding towards us.

Next moment he is looming right over us, a giant shadow blotting out the sun. He is so close I can feel the breeze as he swings his huge ears to keep cool in the hot African sun. Then, with a gentleness surprising for so large an animal, he extends the prehensile tip of his trunk and takes the pods from Alan's fingers.

'It's hard to believe this is a truly wild elephant, isn't it?' says Alan, with a smile of contentment. 'He's so powerful he could snuff us out in one go; yet he's as gentle as a lamb.'

It wasn't always so. Until the 1970s the elephants that roamed this land at the edge of the great Hwange park were ruthlessly persecuted. They had been hunted since the Victorian days of Frederick Courtenay Selous, who pursued elephants on horseback. The herd bulls were dubbed 'rogues' by the ignorant, and big-game hunters shot them, to be photographed astride their gigantic corpses as if to compensate for their own inadequacies.

Like so much of Africa, the Hwange bush country was a bloody killing field for hunters and ivory poachers alike. Alan talks about man as 'the upright ape, the ultimate predator', for so long the elephants' most feared and hated enemy, who initiated them into the cruel law of survival. Long experience had taught them how to respond to the sight of humans. There were only two options: charge or flee.

Says Elliott: 'One of the saddest sights in Africa is to see an elephant running away because it is terrified of man. I was determined that here, at least, the elephants would be able to set aside their fear and live their lives without stress.'

It wasn't easy. In Zimbabwe, the last stronghold of the ivory trade, Elliot is considered something of a maverick. It took him twenty years to protect his elephants. Now, as he had demonstrated so dramatically, he has them literally eating out of his hand.

Yet he is no sentimental bunny-hugger. A tough, bear-like man in the John Wayne mould, he is now in his middle fifties, a fourth-generation Rhodesian who grew up in the bush with the local Matebele children (he speaks their language fluently), and dreamed of becoming a professional elephant hunter. But early on in his career as a district officer, when he had to shoot his first tusker, an old crop-raider, he was overcome by feelings of shame and sadness.

In the early 1970s, with the building of the Hwange Safari Lodge and the birth of tourism in the area, attitudes to wildlife began to change. Zimbabwe Sun Hotels bought miles of bush to create a large private sanctuary at the edge of the national park, and set up a team of guides to escort guests on photo safaris.

The man in charge was the legendary Johnny Uys, a former Zambian Chief Game Warden. Tragically, Uys was killed by an elephant while escorting a group of German tourists. The Germans thought it was all a show and applauded.

Uys died in 1973, and Elliott took over. 'Living in Johnny's shadow wasn't easy,' he said, 'but it was a tremendous challenge.'

When he started, there were just twenty-two frightened elephants. Now there are more than 300 and their fear of man has gone. 'They know they're safe,' said Elliott. 'Our wild estate is the safest place for elephants in Zimbabwe, and maybe in the whole of Africa.'

But what would become of the elephants if anything happened to him? 'This was a worry I've been turning over in my mind for some time,' he said. 'I wanted to find a way of ensuring that they would still be able to roam free long after I was gone.'

It was Ahmed, the giant tusker of Marsabit Mountain in northern Kenya, that gave Elliott the idea. Back in the 1970s, the late President Kenyatta had issued a decree protecting Ahmed. In effect it made the old bull a living national treasure which nobody could shoot without bringing down the wrath of the President on his shoulders.

If Kenya could do it, thought Elliott, then why not Zimbabwe? But this time it was not one elephant but an entire herd that needed protection.

In 1990 he approached Zimbabwe's President, Robert Mugabe; and to his great delight Mugabe agreed. Since then the herd has become, in effect, the President's elephants. 'Thanks to that decision,' said Elliott, 'these elephants will never again have to justify their existence with their blood and their ivory.'

Having fed the bull its seedpods, we drove on through shady woodlands of Zimbabwe teak towards a waterhole not far from Dete Vlei. The *vlei* is a long, shallow, grassy valley — the best place in Africa for seeing sable antelope — and Elliott's own safari company, called, appropriately, Touch the Wild, has two luxury lodges there.

On our way to the waterhole I asked him about the philosophy behind his safari business. 'Why Touch the Wild?' he said. 'Because that's exactly what I wanted people to do. In the bush you must use all your senses. You must look and listen and learn afresh how to reach out to nature. When you do the rewards are endless; and only then will you begin to understand Africa.'

He stopped the vehicle in a clearing and picked the dried seedhead of a wild basil plant, which he crushed in his hand and invited me to sniff. It smelled strongly of camphor. 'The Africans use it when they have a cold,' he said. 'It's all part of touching the wild.'

Farther on he stopped again where fresh elephant spoor crossed the track, and showed me the old hunter's trick of judging the height of a bull by measuring its footprints. He placed a length of string around the circumference of the print left by elephant's front foot, then stretched it straight. 'Double that and you know how tall the bull stands at the shoulder.' he said.

We drove on, drifting slowly through the sunlit woods until we reached the waterhole. A dozen elephants were drinking and bathing in the shallows, accompanied by a forty-year-old matriarch; but Elliott kept his distance. 'I don't like to go too close at this time of day,' he said. 'It's not good to chivvy them out of the shade. Tolerance is a golden rule. They will always repay you by allowing you to drive closer another time.'

We parked the Land-Cruiser in a patch of shade and sat down to wait. The elephants, having drunk their fill, moved off slowly into the combretum. A solitary kudu appeared at the water's edge. A saddlebill stork stood on the far bank.

Towards sundown a large breeding herd arrived, and Alan gently eased the Land-Cruiser forward until we were right among them. His enthusiasm for elephant watching has not diminished with the years. "Look at their trunks. It's like a snakepit,' he exclaimed as the herd surrounded our vehicle and began to drink.

One young bull advanced and began to playfully twirl his trunk around the radio aerial. 'Hey, don't break that,' cried Alan, giving the youngster a slap with his hat. 'Wonderful animals, aren't they?' he said. 'They have become our ambassadors. They create enormous goodwill for Zimbabwe. And in tourist terms they prove their economic worth every day.'

The sky turned red and the elephants departed, but we stayed on, talking quietly. Alan told me about his other enterprises: his new lodge among the bald granite domes of the Matobo Hills, where black eagles soar over the grave of Cecil Rhodes; and his camp at Makalolo in the remote heart of Hwange, a magical spot in winter when the ordeal trees turned to gold and the keening of jackals carried far in the night air. 'Lots of lion; lots of elephants; buffalo and leopard too,' he said. At night when the moon was full and the Kalahari sands shone white as snow, he would follow the lions as they hunted buffalo and wildebeest on the open pans. Of all the wild places in Africa, he said, this was his favourite; and tomorrow he would take me there.

Makalolo — the San bushman name for the rain tree — is a million acres of private wilderness where the boundless spirit of vanishing Africa still breathes among the golden grasslands and iron-grey anthills.

Alan's camp is built around the fallen wreck of a massive, 300-year-old camelthorn acacia tree at the edge of the Samavundhla Pan, an amphitheatre of open parkland with a large waterhole at its centre.

In twenty years of safaris it is the finest bush camp I have ever found. There are no frills; no pool, no gift shop. But what Makalolo offers is more than adequate: a roomy tent, a warm bed, hot showers and three square meals a day, served in a thatched dining room with a campfire and viewing platform overlooking the plain.

At Makalolo the bush is still timeless, untamed, teeming with game. Every day sees a constant procession of animals moving across the pan: zebras, wildebeest, eland, sable, giraffes and elephants. Every night the air carries the hacksaw cough of prowling leopards, the eerie voices of hyenas.

It is the kind of camp where, if you hear lions roaring in the middle of dinner as we did, you can drop everything and drive out to look for them with a halogen spotlight.

Over breakfast next morning Alan told me how he first stumbled on the campsite in 1980.

'I was tracking buffalo in thick bush. It was very hot and at midday I came upon this incredible old camelthorn. Everything else was grey, but the tree was green and it cast a huge pool of shade. The Rhodesian War had just ended and there were still dissidents in the bush. Life in Hwange was still very tricky; but the tree was in flower and the bees were buzzing and the whole place was so peaceful that I decided I would come back and build a camp there one day.'

Some years after he had built the camp, the tree fell down one night, missing him by inches.

Breakfast over, we headed in the direction of Ngamo Plain, a miniature Serengeti where lions and wildebeest and bat-eared foxes live. Its San bushman name means 'the place that glitters from afar'.

On the way there we passed a leadwood tree with the carcase of a steenbok hanging from its branches. The steenbok is a foxy red antelope scarcely bigger than a jackal. Normally they are skilled at concealment, but this one had been discovered and killed by a leopard during the night.

We drove on through arid patches of Kalahari scrub, past shady umtshibi trees and squat baobabs like temple columns, holding up the sky. At noon we stopped for a picnic at the edge of a pan. A herd of sable stared at us from a safe distance in the withered grass. Beyond, the flat horizon was as wide as an ocean, rimmed with tall mlala palms.

'It's dry now,' said Alan, waving a chicken drumstick at the arid landscape, 'but in summer these pans are covered with a foot of water. It's like the Okavango. You'd never recognise it. Blue waterlilies everywhere. Storks in their thousands, and wild duck swimming across the roads.'

We were back in camp in time for dinner and we set out afterwards on a night drive and ran into five lionesses hunting under the stars. Later we found the two Makololo pride males drinking at the waterhole. They were both eight years old and in their prime; one with a blond mane and one with a ginger one.

Thirsts quenched, they rose to their feet and Blond Mane came padding boldly towards our open vehicle. 'Naughty,' said Alan, as if chastising a wayward child. 'Go away.' He waved his hand and the lion stood still, then turned to rejoin its companion.

Up at dawn the following day we set out again and almost at once picked up the tracks of a big male lion — possibly one of the pair we had watched the previous night. Against the light his deep pugmarks were clear to read. Filled with early morning shadow, they lay in the sand like soft, blue flowers.

'They're so fresh,' Alan said. 'Only minutes old. Let's see if we can find him. He can't be far away.' He parked the Land-Cruiser and reached for his rifle. 'Always carry insurance,' he said.

We trod quietly, following the lion's tracks in the cold, still morning. They led down an elephant path, winding through tall yellow grass and autumn-coloured thickets that looked like English hazel coppice.

Twice Alan froze, one hand lifted in warning. Each time I stared into the tangled scrub ahead, wondering if the lion was in there. My ears strained to catch the slightest sound. But all I could hear above the beating of my heart was the clucking of hornbills and the far-off blare of an elephant.

Ahead the bush grew even thicker, cutting down vision to a few metres. 'Time to turn back,' Alan whispered. 'No point in going on. We wouldn't get much of a view of him. We could walk right into him and never know he was there.'

Surely, I thought on the long drive back to camp, not even Makalolo could produce anything more dramatic than tracking lions on foot. But I was wrong.

At sundown, that magical time when the trees turn black against the red Zimbabwe sky, when the francolins begin to call and the air grows cool, we left the Land-Cruiser by the side of the road, took a couple of beers from the cool-box and climbed on to an anthill to listen to the sound of the day winding down.

For an hour we sat there, revelling in the magic of a world at peace while the darkness closed in around us. Nobody spoke. To have done so would have broken the spell.

Then Alan nudged my elbow. Lost in reverie, I had not noticed the arrival of a lone bull elephant. Six tons of silence, striding towards us on huge, cushioned feet. Twenty yards away he stopped and raised his trunk to sift the air for our scent. Then, with a sudden, admonitory shake of his enormous ears, he strode past us and vanished into the night.

The day after leaving Makalolo I flew to Bulawayo and drove up into the Matobo Hills, which lie about twenty miles south of the city in the heart of Matabeleland Province. Alan's stories of the area and its special place in the history of the Matabele people had aroused my curiosity. Now I was determined to see it for myself, which was how I came to be standing on what felt like the roof of southern Africa with half of Zimbabwe at my feet.

The Matabele call it Malindidzimu — 'the Place of Spirits'. To Cecil John Rhodes, the founder of Rhodesia, whose body is buried on its barren summit, it was 'the World's View'. Both names are valid. At Rhodes's grave, on one of the highest points in the Matobo Hills, you look out over a tumbledown landscape cast in granite 2,000 million years ago. In every direction, weathered pinnacles and dizzy rock castles stretch to the horizon, presiding over a chaos of boulder-strewn valleys, as if God had gathered up all the odd lumps of granite left over when the world was complete and scattered them over 1,200 square miles of Matabeleland.

Some hills are nothing but colossal whalebacks of rock. Others resemble the ruins of lost cities, with boulders balanced precariously on top of each other like children's bricks. One shove, you feel, could send the whole lot crashing.

It was in the Matobos that Robert Baden-Powell, then an army colonel, received the inspiration to form the Boy Scout movement; but the whole area, with its sacred caves and prehistoric rock paintings, has a far deeper significance for the Matabele. For them, these strange, brooding hills are still a holy place. King Mzilikazi, their first great leader, is buried here. To Mzilikazi the domed hills looked like a huddle of bald heads, hence the name Matobo.

A hundred years ago the British fought and died here in a series of bloody skirmishes with King Lobengula's impis. Lobengula, who was Mzilikazi's son, had made a treaty with Cecil Rhodes. Too late, he discovered that Rhodes was a cheat. By then he had signed away his kingdom. Driven from Bulawayo, his royal capital, the king led his men into the Matobos, where they hid in caves, waging guerrilla war on the white invaders until his death in 1896.

Now the Matobos are at peace again, with nothing but the cry of a black eagle or the cough of a wandering leopard to disturb the silence of Lobengula's granite kingdom.

Leopards are common here. The Matobos are said to hold a greater concentration than anywhere else in Africa; but they are seldom seen. Among the tumbled rocks and tangled thickets are a million places where a leopard might hide. The closest I came to seeing one was finding the fresh tracks of a big male near the Matobo Hills Lodge.

Likewise, one should not expect to see lions, elephants or buffaloes. Although Matobo is now a national park it is not classic big game country. It is, however, a wonderful place for antelope: sable and kudu, impala and tsessebe, and fleet-footed klipspringers clattering on tiptoe over the rocks.

It has also recently been declared an IPZ — an Intensive Protection Zone for the endangered rhino. Here, far from the Zambian poachers who slip across the Zambezi, Zimbabwe's rhinos will make their last stand.

For a few unforgettable days I shared these hills with the rhinos and klipspringers and the ghosts of Lobengula's warriors, exploring the park with Ian MacDonald, who runs the Matobo Hills Lodge and has known the area all his life.

The rains had ended in early January — a month earlier than normal — and would not return until November. The bush was parched, the grass yellow. The days were hot, the sky a cloudless blue. But the nights were as sharp as a driven nail, bringing five degrees of frost by dawn.

One morning we scrambled over a pile of boulders to reach an overhanging cliff whose smooth granite surface had been used as a canvas by the long-vanished San bushmen. Here, captured in red ochre, was a whole cavalcade of running animals: zebras, a warthog, the horned head of a tsessebe, a man spearing a scrub hare, and a big cat — perhaps a leopard — attacking a hunter.

The pictures looked as fresh as if the unknown artists had only just left. It was the strangest sensation. Ten thousand years had passed and nothing had changed. I sat on the same ledge as they must have done, feeling the same sun on my back. And when I turned round there were more animals, only these were real; a herd of sable moving through the golden grass in the valley below.

Above the cliff face lay a cave, its upper chamber lit by a long shaft of light from somewhere even higher. On the floor of the cave stood a row of rough red clay bins, each one big enough to hide a man. Empty now except for the dried droppings of wild cats and porcupines, they had once stored Matabele grain when Lobengula's warriors hid out in the hills a century ago.

It was an impressive spot. But MacDonald knew a better one, he said; a much bigger cave with wonderful paintings in the Toghwe Wilderness Area.

We set off next day, leaving our Land-Rover at the Toghwana Dam and continuing on foot. Lost in a lonely world of granite, we scrambled over boulders as big as bungalows, following a dry watercourse. In the rainy season it would be impassable, a raging torrent.

On we climbed, past the dead grey husks of the resurrection bush, which would burst into life when the rains returned. At one point MacDonald picked up a lump of slag from a primitive smelter where Iron Age smiths had forged tools and weapons, maybe 1,000 years ago.

Farther on he pointed out a black eagles' eyrie on a dizzy cliff ledge. The black eagle is one of Africa's most spectacular birds of prey and the Matobos are their stronghold, with more than fifty breeding pairs.

'Some of these nest sites have been occupied for centuries,' MacDonald said. 'I wouldn't be surprised if they were nesting here when the smiths were still making their iron weapons.'

From the wind-blown summits of the lofty whalebacks we looked down into a succession of secret valleys, each one thick with yellow grass, the haunt of sable and white rhino.

Underfoot, the rough granite felt wonderfully secure; yet I could see where the rock had peeled and cracked under the endless cycle of sun and frost. 'When the sun is hot the whole mountain expands,' said MacDonald. 'At night, when it cools, it contracts and cracks.'

At last we reached our destination, a great hollow in the side of a cliff, like one half of an inverted dome covered with the now familiar outlines of matchstick men with bows and arrows pursuing giraffes, zebras, kudu and eland, all as vivid as the day they were painted.

As we left the cave we passed the track of a large snake leading down into a dark crevice. 'It's very fresh,' said MacDonald. 'It must have gone in as we approached. Probably a mamba. There's lots in these hills. The locals would tell you it's the guardian of the cave.'

It was dark by the time we got back to the lodge and the African sky was hung with stars. It was the night when the planet Jupiter was about to be struck by a giant comet.

When the moment approached I went outside and stared through my binoculars into deep space. There was Jupiter. The air was so clear that I could even see its moons.

Was it my imagination, or did the planet really grow brighter when the comet struck? I cannot say. What I do know is that, with uncanny precision, at the very moment of impact, all the jackals of the Matobos began to cry, their keening voices rising and falling in the cold night air.

Chapter Eleven
Between the Desert and the Sea

There was no road to Purros. Only the ruts of old tyre tracks disappearing westward into the mountains and deserts of Kaokoland. Purros itself was nothing but a scattering of shacks and mud huts belonging to the Himba, nomadic pastoralists who dress in skins and roam the ochre hills with their goats and cattle.

As we lurched down the dried-up bed of the Gomatum River, a tributary of the Hoarusib, the sky turned black and thunder rumbled in the hills. 'Is it going to rain?' I asked. Sitting at the wheel of his Toyota Land-Cruiser, my companion, the photographer David Coulson, shook his head. 'Not here,' he said positively. 'Not in the desert.'

Coulson should know, I thought. He had been travelling around Namibia for years. But even as he spoke the first fat spots began to fall. Moments later we were in the midst of a ferocious tropical storm — and it was precisely then that fate decided we should have a puncture. We were already late. There was nothing for it but to leap out into the lashing rain and change the wheel.

Within seconds we were soaked to the skin. When at last the wheel was fixed I took off my desert boots and poured the water out of them. 'I thought you said this was a bloody desert,' I said. It was an odd way to begin what turned out to be the hottest weeks of my life in one of the driest, emptiest and most inaccessible places on earth.

Namibia is the last great wilderness in southern Africa. Imagine a country four times the size of Britain with fewer than 1.2 million people. Much of the land is desert. Some of its rivers do not run for years. In some places no rain has fallen this century.

To explore such harsh terrain requires local expertise. That is why we were heading to Purros, to rendezvous with Louw and Amy Schoeman, who were going to take us on a safari to the Skeleton Coast.

The Skeleton Coast National Park is a strip of desert up to 25 miles wide, running for some 300 miles from the Cunene River on the Angolan border down to the Ugab River near Cape Cross. In 1971, when the park was proclaimed, it was decided to set aside the northern sector as a wilderness area where only limited tourism would be allowed. In 1977 it was Schoeman, a practising attorney and one-time diamond prospector turned tour operator, who was awarded the concession to operate fly-in safaris there. Since then he had flown, driven and walked all over the area, and come to know it better than anyone.

'Never underestimate the desert,' he said. 'It isn't hostile but it can be dangerous — even deadly if you don't know it. But I've been coming here for thirty years and it's just like moving around in my own living room. I love it. I really do. I think it's one of the most beautiful places on earth.'

From Purros we followed Schoeman across country, traversing immense gravel plains with no sign of life except a few springbok and ostrich on the farthest horizons, until we came at sunset to his camp on the edge of the Khumib River. The river had flowed a month ago after heavy storms in the mountains up country, said Louw; but now it was bone dry again.

The mess tent was set up under the spreading branches of an ancient omumborumbonga or leadwood, the holy tree of the Herero people. At suppertime shy, spotted genets emerged from its branches to wait for scraps.

When I went to bed I fancied I could smell the sea on the night breeze, although the coast was a good eight miles away; and sure enough, when I awoke in the stillness of dawn I could hear the roar of the Atlantic surf, like the distant drumroll of a passing jet-liner.

After breakfast, before we set out, I was given a hat, a legionnaire-style képi with a flap to protect the back of my neck from the desert sun, although Schoeman himself always went hatless, even on the hottest days. With his grey hair and avuncular manner he had the look of a country doctor; but in reality he was one of Namibia's most experienced desert veterans, possessed of an endless store of knowledge gleaned from the barren world about us.

'We're paranoid about vehicle tracks up here,' said Louw as we set out through the dune-fields towards the sea. 'The desert is a fragile place, easy to scar and slow to heal. I can show you tracks made in 1943 to rescue survivors from the wreck of the *Dunedin Star*. Even now they look as if they were made only last week; and there are other areas, on the coarser, more stable gravel plains, where tyre tracks will last for centuries.'

We drove on through an expanse of barchan dunes — wandering sandhills which crawl across the desert floor before the prevailing southerly winds at the rate of as much as 100 feet a year. At first glance these shifting sands seem utterly devoid of life; yet every slope bears a scribble of prints — signatures left by lizards, side-winder snakes and fog beetles which collect the dew that condenses on their backs.

In places the sands are stained a rich maroon, as if someone had emptied giant vats of claret down the slopes. Louw handed me a magnifying glass and told me to take a closer look. With my nose in the sand I squinted through the glass and discovered that each polished grain was in fact a miniature gemstone. I was lying on a bed of garnets!

With Louw I learned the secret of driving in dune-fields. You simply let down the tyres until they are like squashy balloons. Then, with the vehicle in four-wheel drive, you put your foot down and float through the soft sand with a sensation akin to skiing in powder snow.

As we came up over the last crest of sand there was the glorious sight of the Atlantic below, green and white rollers crashing on an empty shore and a cool breeze coming in from the sea.

Offshore, two trawlers were rising and falling in the swell. 'Spanish, probably,' said Louw. 'They've robbed this country of billions of pounds of fish.'

The beach was knee-deep in spume; an extraordinary phenomenon produced by the rich blooms of plankton which thrive in the cold Benguela Current. Whipped up by the surf to the consistency of shaving cream, it lay on the shore in thick, quivering fields, slowly breaking up in the wind to roll away like tumbleweed.

Up and down the coast as far as the eye can see, the sands were littered with the flotsam of centuries; a tangle of ships' masts, planks and spars, with here and there the bleached skeleton of a great whale, butchered by the American whaling fleets a hundred years ago. Kelp gulls watched at a distance and ghost crabs danced away over the sands on tiptoe like fleeting shadows; but ours were the only footprints.

The following day we flew over the Skeleton Coast on our way north to the Cunene, where Schoeman had another camp looking across the river into Angola. Below us were scattered more masts, more ribs and vertebrae and giant jawbones of the vanished whales. We flew low over a colony of Cape fur seals hauled out on the beach, and narrowly missed a flock of rare Damara terns which rose from the water like a white cloud in front of us. Had we hit them it would have brought down our small aircraft as effectively as any ground-to-air missile, but Schoeman appeared unperturbed. I learned later that among his friends he was known as 'low-flying Schoeman.'

At last we came to the wide brown mouth of the Cunene and followed it inland across a scene of utter desolation. To the south lay nothing but the glare of salt pans, a terrifying emptiness reaching away into the dunes and mountain ranges of Kaokoland. To the north rose the sun-scorched rocks of Angola. 'Amazing to think that most of this country we've been flying over has never had a human foot on it,' Schoeman yelled above the engine's roar. 'Not even a bushman.'

It seemed impossible that there could be any safe place to land in this burnt and broken country; but eventually a strip appeared and we touched down on a wide plain to step out into the blow-torch heat of late afternoon.

A vehicle was waiting to take us to Louw's camp. Recent rains had raised a brief flush of green grass from the red sand, but already it was withering in the fierce heat. To the south, a range of nameless hills raised their granite heads. Rock kestrels whistled among the crags, and larks flew up as we drove along the stony ridges in search of a safe place to descend to the river, but their cries were torn away on the hot wind.

By the time we reached camp the sun was setting. Shadows seeped out of the ground like smoke, filling the hollows of the hills above the gorge in which the river hissed and swirled in spate. There was a swimming pool among the rocks (the river itself was full of crocodiles), and although there was barely room enough to turn round, it was bliss to cool off and then sit with a cold beer and watch the lightning flickering in the mountains of Angola.

Somewhere up there in those forbidding hinterlands, the Cunene has its source in the same giant watershed which gives rise to the Zambezi and the Okavango. But unlike them, the Cunene flows westward to the Atlantic, forming one of the loneliest frontiers on earth.

'You don't come here to see animals,' said Schoeman. 'It's not like the Etosha National Park. You come for the remoteness, the ruggedness. That's what the Cunene is all about. Mass tourism has no place here; but a few people will pay for the privilege of coming to such a wild area, and they need the kind of guidance we can provide. It's not a good place to get stuck in.'

Next morning, Schoeman launched an inflatable boat powered by two giant outboard engines, and we set off upstream, bumping over the racing brown current in which whirlpools spun and sinister up-wellings gurgled under our bows. After about a mile the gorge began to narrow and the water became even more turbulent, tumbling towards us in a series of roaring rapids. Here the river did its best to unseat us, but we clung on grimly as the boat bucked and turned beneath our feet.

Ahead rose towering granite walls, closing in like the gates of hell. Somehow we squeezed through them and surged on between a chaos of sunless cliffs which had collapsed like a stack of giant dominoes, until our way was blocked by an enormous cataract and we could go no further.

Once we were out of the rapids, returning downstream was far more enjoyable. Goliath herons flapped out of the reed-beds and brilliant green and yellow bee-eaters sat on the swaying branches of the winterthorn trees above luxuriant tangles of morning glory flowers.

Back at camp we lazed over a late breakfast, then left the Cunene to fly back to the Khumib. Once more that savage northern landscape unfolded beneath our wings, the sands a smouldering Martian red, the blinding soda pans, the mountains flayed bare by wind and sun. I was glad I had been to the Cunene, but at the same time I felt relieved to be escaping from its brooding hostility.

At the Khumib we made our farewells to Louw and Amy Schoeman, bump-started Coulson's Land-Cruiser and set off south down the Skeleton Coast. I did not know that I would never see this remarkable man again. Sadly, Louw died of a heart attack in 1993.

After an hour or so we came to the mouth of the Hoarusib. There had been more storms inland and the river was running. We waded across it to see if it was too deep to drive. The water was still below our knees but flowing strongly and rising as we watched, coming down in sudden surges that spread out across the sand. It was now or never. We could not afford to wait. Slowly we nosed into the flood and drove across it obliquely with the water lapping at the bottom of the doors, but the riverbed was firm and we had no difficulty in reaching the other side.

It was now late afternoon. Down on the shore, bathed in the golden Atlantic light, springbok were feeding. It seemed incongruous to find them beside the sea. Sometimes, said Coulson, desert-dwelling elephants followed the sand rivers down to the coast, leaving their giant footprints along the beach; and from time to time a desert lion would come wandering out of Damaraland to scavenge for seal carcases in the surf.

Our destination was the ranger station at Mowe Bay, where we stayed two nights with Rod Braby, the principal nature conservation officer for the Skeleton Coast Park, and Sigi, his German-born wife. With its bleached driftwood shacks and small gardens heaped with fish nets, whalebones, elephant skulls and other flotsam, the bleak little settlement was like the setting for a Steinbeck novel.

Yet despite its remoteness it seemed to attract a succession of the most remarkable and gifted people. One of the shacks was the home of the wildlife film-makers Des and Jen Bartlett, who had spent the past fourteen years living and working in the Namibian parks. Over a breakfast of tea and kippers they explained how they had been using microlight aircraft to film for the first time the desert-dwelling elephants as they migrated through the dunes.

Later we met Garth Owen Smith, the tall, bearded desert veteran who has done more than anyone to protect the elephants of Damaraland and Kaokoland, and his colleague, Rudi Loutit, who has been fighting to save the last of Namibia's desert rhinos.

Loutit's latest project involved dehorning the rhinos to deny the poachers the prize they sought. 'People were very defeatist when we started,' he said. 'They said the rhinos would be killed by lions if we removed their horns. I think a lot of this talk was just pique. Anyway, we went ahead and did it, because we've got to get these wonderful animals into the next century, and it's been a great success.'

He paused, a dark, good-looking man in his green ranger's uniform. 'You know, my wife Blythe and I never had any kids because of the life we lead. We decided to dedicate ourselves to keeping the rhino alive, and it's ironic, really. We're keeping them alive for other people's kids to see.'

After Rudi had gone I went down to the shore, sat on the beach and thought about these extraordinary and solitary men who had lived for so long in the wilderness and were now themselves a vanishing species.

A fog bank came rolling in, heavy with the smell of kelp. The damp sea mist clung to my bare legs but I was not cold. I walked for miles, relieved to be out of the desert heat, listening to the gulls which reminded me of home, beachcombing for agate pebbles among the jackal prints and sea-urchin shells

It was hard to believe I was still in Africa, yet I knew that inland, less than five miles away, the sky would be a burning blue and the sand underfoot too hot to tread on.

We left the Skeleton Coast Park at its southern end below the Ugab River. A ranger opened the gates, adorned with sinister black-painted skulls and cross-bones, and we followed the Atlantic down to Swakopmund, a clean, cool oasis of palm trees and old-fashioned buildings still dreaming of the Kaiser's Germany.

Swakopmund provided a brief interlude of hot baths, clean sheets and air-conditioned rooms. Then we were off once more to the desert, following the bone-dry Kuiseb River into the Namib–Naukluft National Park.

This was the true Namib — 'the Place where there is Nothing' — a sunstruck wilderness of gravel plains above which mirages of distant mountain-tops appeared as rocky islands in a trembling sea of blue.

High, rolling dunes marched south with us down the western horizon, like the Sussex Downs painted red. Further south at Sossusvlei these dunes reach a height of 1,000 feet — the tallest in the world. There was no water anywhere, but there were trees beside the Kuiseb riverbed, giant winterthorns from whose broad parasols of shade had fallen large seedpods with furry shells as soft as moleskin.

Here we camped at a place called Homeb, and when it was cooler in late afternoon we crossed the riverbed and climbed up out of the valley to watch the sun go down behind the dunes. We came to a stony plateau scattered with wind-blasted pebbles of clear white and yellow crystal which glittered in the sand like fallen stars. Nothing grew here except for a few sparse grey tufts of grass that creaked and hissed in the wind; yet scatterings of old, dry spoor showed that gemsbok and zebra had passed this way.

Back in camp, night came swiftly. A full moon arose. In the clear desert air, every detail of its cratered surface was visible through my binoculars. We barbecued the steaks we had bought in Swakopmund and ate them with potatoes and onions wrapped in foil and baked in the embers, washed down with beers from the cool-box.

Later, stretched out in my sleeping bag, I lay on my back looking up at the brightest stars in Africa. The bushmen, who believe the stars to be hunters in the heavens, say they can hear them in the deep silence of the desert; but I could hear only the sepulchral hoot of an owl somewhere down river, and the jackals crying in the dunes. The last thing I remembered before I fell asleep was that this was Easter Sunday.

Above Homeb the course of the river cuts through a range of cindery hills into the desolate Kuiseb canyonlands where two Germans, Hermann Korn and Henno Martin, and their palindromic dog, Otto, hid for nearly three years to avoid being interned by the South Africans during the Second World War.

Above: Kariba sunset; one of the glories of a visit to Zimbabwe's Matusadona national park. The trees were drowned when the Zambezi Valley was flooded to create the lake. *(Brian Jackman)*

Left: Oxpecker on buffalo. Oxpeckers rid their hosts of ticks and also alert the animals to possible danger. *(Jonathan Scott)*

Top: The President's elephants: part of the herd protected by President Robert Mugabe of Zimbabwe. 'Never again will these elephants have to justify their existence with their blood and their ivory.' *(Brian Jackman)*

Bottom: Cape fur seal colony near Sandwich Bay on Namibia's lonely Skeleton Coast. *(David Coulson)*

'If Etosha has a totem it is surely the haughty gemsbok, with its startling black and white face, like an African tribal mask, and its extraordinary ability to go for months on end without drinking.' *(David Coulson)*

Top: Zebras drinking at Fischer's Pan, in Etosha national park near Namutoni. *(David Coulson)*

Bottom: Red Lechwe antelope in the Okavango Delta. Only when you fly over the Okavango does its sheer scale and size sink in. *(David Coulson)*

Later, Henno Martin recounted the story of their Robinson Crusoe existence in a book, *The Sheltering Desert*, in which he graphically describes their solitary lives, shooting game, searching for water in the bottom of the canyons and coming to terms with the hardships imposed by one of the cruellest places on earth.

We visited one of their old hide-outs, the place they called Carp Cliff, high above the Kuiseb Canyon. Here the two fugitives had built a shelter under the overhanging rim rock, living like Neolithic man on whatever game they could catch. The walls they had built fifty years ago were still there, and a stone slab they had used as a table. Mountain zebras had come this way not long ago. We found fresh spoor at the foot of the cliff and I remembered Henno Martin's accounts of how he and Hermann would shoot zebra and gemsbok, turn the meat into biltong, make the blood into sausages and sometimes enjoy a nostalgic feast of gemsbok liver dumplings and sauerkraut in the middle of the desert.

Distance lends these far-reaching barrenlands a surreal perspective, with the sharkfin shapes of mountain ranges thrusting over faraway horizons. Here, in the pitiless heat of the Namib, the earth's rocks are being tested to destruction, blow-torched by the sun, sand-blasted by the searing winds, broken down into fissured gullies and ravines in which the eye cries out for the sight of a green tree or a pool of water. In the emptiness of the Namib the earth is already a dying planet. This is the shape of things to come. Long after mankind and all other life has been extinguished from the face of the world, the inert carcase of this implacable desert will continue to roll on through space.

All my life I have loved wilderness and wild places, but the Namib's unrelenting hostility defeated me. In its furnace heat I could feel my spirit wilting like a dying flower. Only in the last golden hour before sunset and again in the first cool hour of dawn does the desert relent, allowing deep shadows to soften its harsh contours, transforming it into a silent world of unearthly beauty.

On the way back to Swakopmund, driving through the burnt-out badlands and labyrinthine canyons of the Swakop River, we came to a stony valley upon whose slopes grew hundreds of *Welwitschia mirabilis*, one of the world's oldest and weirdest plants. Some of these living botanical fossils are said to be 1,500 years old; yet in their entire lifetime they produce only two leaves, which may reach a length of up to nine feet and split into long, leathery green fronds. I did not care for the welwitschias. They lie in the sun like something out of John Wyndham's *Day of the Triffids*, as if waiting to shoot out one of their sinister-looking leaves to grab you by the ankle, suck out your juices and then discard you like an empty paper bag.

Next day we drove down from Swakopmund into the South African enclave of Walvis Bay to meet Ernst Karlowa, the Skeleton Coast Park's first warden.

Now in his seventies, he lives quietly in a Walvis Bay suburb, tending the flowers in his oasis of a garden which is so different from the inhospitable shores where he spent most of his life.

'Until 1960 the coast and its hinterland was still an impenetrable wilderness, even with four-wheel drive,' he said. 'In Afrikaans we call it the "*Seekus van die Dood*" — "the Sea Coast of the Dead". I spent three years alone up there. Sometimes it felt like solitary confinement, the wind howling and the camp moaning and creaking like a ship at sea. I'd never do it again. It's a hard land, and yet after a while it takes hold of you and you find it hard to let go.'

In 1974, patrolling by Land-Rover in the dunes near False Cape Fria, Karlowa made one of the most exciting discoveries of his life. 'At first I thought it was an old wooden pulley lying among some ship's timbers. I picked it up and found myself staring into this mysterious, enigmatic face. It set me back on my heels, I can tell you.'

What Karlowa had found was the carved wooden face of a ship's figurehead, almost certainly a sixteenth century galleon, possibly Spanish but probably Portuguese, one of hundreds of nameless ships cast up on the Sea Coast of the Dead. It lies now in the small private museum of the ranger post at Mowe Bay; one of Africa's most moving relics, gathering dust in a desert shack.

Afterwards, a pilot friend of David Coulson's volunteered to take us for one last look at the Skeleton Coast before I returned to England the next day. We took off in his four-seater Cessna and flew down the coast to Sandwich Bay, an immense shallow lagoon of islands, sand-bars and salt-flats haunted by fleets of pelicans and thousands of flamingoes which took flight as our shadow passed over them and swirled away in pink clouds over the blue water.

Where the surf creamed against the outermost edges of the sandbanks, colonies of Cape fur seals had hauled themselves out of the water to lie in dense, brown packs, staring at the jackals which patrol the shore, waiting to feed on the sick and the dead.

Farther south again we flew over the wreck of the *Eagle*, a nineteenth century barque with her ribs and spars sticking out of the sand. We made a low pass along the beach, the yellow dunes towering above us to landward, the green waves breaking beneath our wheels, then rose until we could see the endless emptiness of the coast reaching all the way to the Orange River, which lay somewhere over the horizon.

By the time we turned for home the flowing summits of the dunes had already begun to glow in the evening light. From the air the Namib and its giant dunescapes appeared as lifeless as the moon. Then came a sight to lift the heart. Out of the shadows a group of gemsbok came galloping, their horns held high like lances, hooves kicking up puffs of sand as they pounded up the smooth incline and cantered away into the setting sun.

Chapter Twelve
Etosha

All day, as we drove north through Hereroland, giant thunderheads had been piling up in the torrid heat, rumbling like lions in the granite hills. Here the summer rains had been good, and all the way from Windhoek the tall roadside grasses rippled in the breeze. Exotic African butterflies — copper-coloured monarchs and huge black and yellow swallowtails — flipped lazily among the ripening panicles. Hornbills looped over the treetops, and the air, washed clean by the rain, sparkled diamond bright above an endless sea of bush.

So far, despite the abundance of life, the goshawks perched on the telegraph poles, the profusion of creamy-white hibiscus flowers and luxuriant creepers, we had seen no game. But ahead lay Etosha, a national park bigger than Switzerland. Etosha is elephant country; the land of the lion and the zebra, home to great herds of antelopes and gazelles and a last stronghold of the black rhino. Long before we had reached the Von Lindequist gate at the park's eastern approaches, I began to scan the surrounding bush, hoping for a glimpse of a horned head in the shadows.

We entered the park and reached the old German fort at Namutoni just as the sun was setting behind the encircling clumps of tall makalani palms. Ever since noon the thunderclouds had been gathering. Now, as they slowly advanced across the plains, trailing dark pillars of rain, the last rays of the sun set them aflame as zebras emerged from the shade of the woodlands to canter in the cooling air.

Swiftly the day's last embers smouldered and died. A thin rind of moon appeared over Namutoni's Beau Geste ramparts, and in no time it was possible to pick out the four-pointed diadem of the Southern Cross suspended in the vast bowl of the night sky. Wrapped once again in the magic of Africa, I found it hard to imagine that I had flown in from Frankfurt only that morning.

Unseen, a scops owl began its insistent trill, and from farther off came the eerie war whoop of a wandering hyena. Somewhere out there beyond the drum-roll of the zebra's hoof beats lay the immense salt pan which is the fierce white heart of Etosha; but that would have to wait until tomorrow

For years I had wanted to visit Etosha, drawn by the breathtaking portraits of its animals captured for television by Des and Jen Bartlett and David Hughes. By now I had seen most of the other great African parks; Etosha was the missing piece of the jigsaw.

For some years Namibia had been a political hot spot as the Swapo guerrillas fought to free their country from South African rule. But now it was March

1991 and the troubles were over. Namibia had been independent for more than a year and Etosha was back in business.

Etosha — 'the Great White Place' — is the ghost of a lake which died twelve million years ago; a shallow, clay-lined depression, 81 miles long and 45 across at its widest point, covered with salt crystals so bright they hurt the eye. For most of the year it is as dead as Mars, a pitiless inferno scoured by dust devils. But during the rains, if the gods are kind, Etosha returns to life. For a few brief weeks it becomes a lake again, a magical place of shimmering reflections, thronged with flamingoes in their tens of thousands, fleets of pelicans and wading birds beyond counting.

All too soon its saline waters are sucked into the hot African sky, leaving fresh encrustations of salt to crack in the unrelenting heat. Yet miraculously, even at the height of the dry season, the surrounding plains and yellowing woodlands conceal artesian springs and permanent waterholes, making Etosha one of the finest wildlife sanctuaries in southern Africa.

It was not until the mid-nineteenth century that the first European trader-explorers managed to penetrate Etosha's pristine fastness, cutting their ox-wagon tracks northwards into Olamboland. Yet already by 1907 the German colonial government of South West Africa was so concerned about the effect of uncontrolled hunting that Etosha became part of an enormous wildlife haven that stretched right across Kaokoland to the Skeleton Coast. Known simply as 'Game Reserve No. 2', it covered nearly 40,000 square miles and was the biggest wildlife refuge in Africa.

At first Etosha's wild herds were free to come and go as they pleased, migrating far beyond the reserve boundaries during the rainy season; but in time, as farmers and ranchers began to erect game-proof fences, the old freedoms were inevitably diminished.

Then, in the 1970s, Etosha suffered a bitter blow. At this time Namibia was still in thrall to South Africa, which set up a commission to establish apartheid homelands for the local people living in the far north. As a result of this deeply controversial 'Odendaal plan', the whole of Kaokoland was deprived of its game reserve status and Etosha was reduced at a stroke to a mere quarter of its original size. However, the 8,600 square miles of wilderness which survived now enjoy full national park status and is still one of Africa's biggest animal strongholds.

Next morning I awoke not to the usual dawn chorus of doves and francolins, but to the brassy notes of a bugle. The old fort may have surrendered to modern tourism, but at sunrise reveille is still sounded from the tower, recalling the days when the black, red and white flag of the Kaiser's Germany fluttered over Namutoni and seven men of the *Schutztruppe* fought off a frenzied attack by 500 heavily armed Ovambo tribesmen.

The air was fresh as we set out. Springbok bounded away across the grass and Cape turtle doves chanted from the treetops. At Klein Namutoni, a deep pool glittered in a glade, fed by an artesian spring which came bubbling out of the encircling calcrete* ridge, and a jackal lay on the far side with eyes half closed, basking in the sun.

But Namutoni's most famous resident, a magnificent black rhino bull known as the Ambassador, was not at home. The Ambassador was at least thirty years old, and had wonderful horns. Like most of Etosha's 300 rhinos, years of poaching had taught him to be secretive and nocturnal in his habits, hiding in thick bush by day and emerging only at night to drink. Now, released by the rains from his dependence on the permanent watering places, he had wandered away into the trackless woodlands in the south of the park.

The glade was starred with yellow flowers, as thick as buttercups in an English meadow, and a flock of grey louries — long-tailed birds with querulous voices and punkish crests — were nibbling at the petals. With the Land-Cruiser parked only a few yards from the water's edge, I sat and watched as a procession of black-faced impala — one of Africa's rarest antelope — trooped in to drink.

Delicately they sniffed the air with their distinctive sooty muzzles. Then, perhaps catching our scent on the fitful breeze, their white tails fluffed out in alarm and they bounded off into the trees. It was a magical encounter. These black-faced impala occur only in northern Namibia. Etosha has a population of about 200, and I must have seen at least sixty of them.

The following day I drove around Fischer's Pan, an almost landlocked bay of salt on the edge of the great Etosha pan itself, just north of Namutoni. The rains had been generous here, leaving parts of the pan still flooded, and large concentrations of game had been drawn to the surrounding plains. In the morning light, zebras were drifting out of the thornbush country, where they spent the night, to feed in the open country. Giraffes stood among the beautiful terminalia trees whose ripe seedpods glowed ox-blood red in the slanting sun, and far out on the flats I could make out long columns of wildebeest strung out like black beads across the grass.

Most handsome of all the grazing animals to my mind were the gemsbok: powerful antelope with sleek café-au-lait bodies and rapier horns which can easily impale a lion. If Etosha has a totem, it is surely the haughty gemsbok with its startling black and white face, like an African tribal mask, and its extraordinary ability to go for months without drinking. Around Namutoni they were everywhere, trotting like lancers along the horizon or charging through the shallows in a welter of spray.

How good it felt to be back in the bush again on one of those glorious golden mornings. In Africa the first and last hours of the day are always the best. The plaintive cries of larks and pipits hung in the wind, and a mother

* Hard, weathered limestone

cheetah with a single yearling cub came treading through the grass, crossing the trail in front of me with barely a backward glance.

Next day, on the way to Halali restcamp, the landscape began to change. Soon the impenetrable bush country where the rhinos hid in their thickets of thorns was left behind. On either side of the dusty white road, tall grasses grew, stretching between the mopane glades. Small groups of hartebeest stood under the trees, and the air was loud with birds, giving these languid woodlands the feel of an English parkland.

Halali is a large camp with a restaurant and a swimming pool in the middle of the mopane country, a few miles below the southern edge of the great Etosha pan. It was built in 1967 at the foot of the Tsumases Kopje, one of the few hills which disturb the flatness of the park's eastern half, and its name, Halali, derives from an old German word describing the blowing of a horn at the end of a hunt.

Early next morning I drove out of Halali, heading north across the plains until I came to the waterhole at Salvadora, on the very edge of the pan. No one else was there. Nor were there any animals to be seen. Apart from a black korhaan* which launched itself into the air with loud heckling cries, there was no sign of life. I looked inland through my binoculars, scanning the flats for the sphinx-like outline of a resting cheetah, but saw only the fleeting shadow of a bat-eared fox slipping through the dawn.

Ahead lay the pan, a desolation of sand and salt crystals reaching out to the edge of the world, above which the sun now rose like a quivering red bubble. Another hour and the pan would become a furnace, a blinding void haunted by cruel mirages. Long before midday the air would turn molten and run rippling along the horizon, causing the receding shores to break away into floating islands, wobbling hilltops and lines of disembodied ostriches dancing over shining lakes. With its aching emptiness and daunting distances it is a fearsome spot. Yet in this first cool hour of dawn, and again in the golden hour before dusk, Etosha pan becomes a place of serene and almost unbearable loveliness.

'There's something special about Etosha,' said Raymond Dujardin, the Head Ranger at Halali. 'It's something to do with the wildness and the dryness that drives the animals together; but above all it is the presence of the pan.'

Dujardin, a tough, grey-haired, chain-smoking Belgian, had once hunted elephants in the Congo. Now he was an ardent conservationist and had spent the past nine years protecting Etosha's animals.

One afternoon he led me down a winding trail to his favourite waterhole. It lay deep in the mopane, in the middle of a wild meadow which few tourists

---

* A southern African species of bustard

ever managed to find. A pair of giraffes watched us from the edge of the woods as we arrived. Zebra stallions were play-fighting and rolling in the grass, sending up clouds of dust, and a lappet-faced vulture sat in a tree, waiting for something to die.

Suddenly the zebras looked up, and we turned to see an enormous bull elephant marching out of the trees to drink. He swayed as he walked, his huge ears spread wide and his trunk swinging to the rhythm of his stride. He drank slowly. A big elephant needs plenty of water — at least twenty five gallons a day — and I could hear his stomach rumbling like a cavernous cistern as he sucked up the water with his trunk and then poured it down his throat in great satisfying draughts.

The sunlight gleamed on his cracked yellow tusks. 'He's old, that one,' whispered Dujardin. 'See how the skin has shrunk around the hollows of his skull.' He was right. This splendid old veteran must have been at least fifty, and I found it poignant to think that he had been wandering across Namibia since the beginning of the Second World War, a living monument at peace with his world.

The sun slid down behind the trees. Sandgrouse began flighting in to alight at the water's edge. The elephant, its thirst satisfied, turned and walked away as soundlessly as it had arrived, a grey ghost fading into the forest; but we stayed on, mesmerised by the beauty of the place and the moment.

There was no doubt about it. Etosha was a glorious wilderness. Yet a nagging impatience gnawned at my enjoyment of its teeming herds and boundless space. I had seen animals galore; elephants and gemsbok and black-faced impala; but where were the lions? There were supposed to be 300 in the park, but so far I had only heard them roaring one night at Namutoni.

I need not have worried. When at last Dujardin and I turned to go, we had not driven more than 100 yards from the edge of the waterhole when we noticed six dark shadows slipping through the grass towards us. Two lionesses were approaching, their coats pale grey in the gathering dusk, with four large cubs, three-quarters grown. Utterly indifferent to our presence, they padded by on either side and fanned out across the meadow. We silenced the engine and from perhaps a mile off heard another lion roaring, its voice trailing off in a series of deep, coughing grunts. I wondered it if was the pride male calling to his companions.

Later, no doubt, they would set an ambush for the zebras; but already it was too dark to see. With bats flitting in the beams of our headlights, we drove back to Halali, leaving the night to the prides of Etosha.

Chapter Thirteen
The Miraculous Oasis

First light in the delta; a mist rising over the reeds and a swelling chorus of Cape turtle doves exhorting the world to 'work harder, work harder'. Later the day would become hot and the herds of impala drinking at the edge of the flood plain would troop back through the yellow grass to seek the shade; but in July these bright Okavango mornings are always cold.

With a boatman called Mighty we had set out from Pom-Pom safari camp to see a twelve-foot-long python which had taken refuge on an island a few miles away. Three weeks earlier, the python had swallowed a red lechwe, a swamp-dwelling antelope, and it had remained on the island ever since, coiled up with a bulge in its middle as it tried to digest its outsize meal.

Now, with an effortless grace born of long experience, Mighty was poling us across Pom-Pom lagoon in a *mokoro*, the traditional Okavango canoe, which is usually carved from the trunk of a sausage tree. Hippos were lying in midstream, filling the air with cavernous chuckles. They rested with only the tops of their heads exposed, snorting and staring with piggy eyes, and Mighty was careful not to stray too close — hippos are responsible for more deaths in Africa than any other animal.

But once past the hippos we relaxed and enjoyed the birds: giant kingfishers with chestnut bellies and polka-dot wings; egrets and pygmy geese; a saddlebill stork skewering frogs in the shallows; and an African fish eagle whose exultant yelping cry followed us across the water.

Silently we glided on down narrow reed canyons, nosing between rafts of mauve-flowering water lilies, heading for the islands whose clumps of fig trees and graceful hyphaene palms stood marooned on the floodplain.

As we drew closer the water became shallower — barely a foot deep in places and almost hidden beneath the tops of the drowned grasses that rose all around us in a green haze. But for the sound of the floodwater under our bows we might have been cruising across a meadow.

It was in these wild waterlands that we surprised a whole herd of lechwe, which raced off in alarm, plunging like porpoises through the deeper channels and then splashing away into the trees. When at last we reached the spot where the python had lain there was nothing but trampled grass and part of a backbone covered with dried blood. It was clear that an epic struggle had taken place, and Mighty was in no doubt what had happened. 'This python has been eaten by a very large crocodile,' he said solemnly.

Top: Shaka Zulu, the king of Shinde Island in the Okavango delta. *(David Coulson)*

Bottom: Shaka Zulu trying to dig a warthog from its burrow. He dug for half an hour but the den was too deep. *(David Coulson)*

Top: On safari with Abu, Randall Moore's favourite riding elephant, taken on Pom-Pom island in 1991. (*Brian Jackman*)

Bottom: Where the grass is as high as an elephant's eye: on safari near Abu's Camp in the Okavango delta. (*Brian Jackman*)

Travelling by *mokoro* is by far the most intimate way of exploring these languid African everglades; but only when you fly over the delta in a five-seater bush plane does its sheer size and scale begin to sink in.

In Maun, the dusty, tin-roofed township on the Thamalakane River which acts as a springboard for all delta safaris, I met Tim Liversedge, a former Botswana game warden and wildlife film-maker who was also an experienced bush pilot. I had first met Tim in London, where I had worked with him on the commentary script of his beautiful film, *March of the Flame Bird*, about the flamingoes of the Makgadikgadi pans. Now he was busy filming one of Africa's rarest birds, Pel's fishing owl, which emerges at dusk like a giant orange moth to drift among the remote ebony groves of the Okavango's swampy heartland; but he had kindly volunteered to take a break from the owls and show me the delta from the air.

We took off from Maun's two-roomed international airport and headed north in Tim's small plane, bouncing from thermal to thermal over the unending flatness of Botswana. At first the ground beneath us resembled an old lion pelt drying in the sun, bare in places, furred with yellow grasses and threaded with game trails. But soon the first gleams of water announced the beginnings of the delta.

Five hundred feet below, the plane's shadow skimmed an infinity of papyrus beds, oxbow lagoons and shining channels; a miraculous oasis spilling for more than 10,000 square miles across the northern Kalahari sands.

The plane droned on. Ahead of us, pelicans were swinging in slow spirals over the treetops, and we banked to avoid them. Shy sitatunga stared up from their marshy couches in the papyrus. Herds of lechwe splashed from island to island, and zebras were trekking through the shallows, following the floods in search of fresh grazing.

The floods come every year, fuelled by summer rains in the Angolan highlands 1,000 miles to the west, where the Okavango has its beginnings. They arrive, paradoxically, in the middle of the dry season, in the winter months of July and August; but then the Okavango has always been an enigma. Most rivers are predictable in their movements: they follow the easiest route to the sea. But the Okavango turns its back on the Atlantic, which is only 180 miles from its source, and strikes out in the opposite direction towards the Indian Ocean, nearly 2,000 miles away.

At first it flows strongly, the third greatest river in southern Africa, with banks 100 yards apart; but once inside Botswana its waters falter. In vain they fan out through the papyrus, seeking a way across the desert to the sea, only to dribble away into the sand or evaporate in the hot African sun.

Sometimes only the northern delta floods; sometimes the south. It all depends on the earthquakes that shiver deep down under the Kalahari sands. The land is so flat that the slightest tremor can tilt the delta floor and upset its delicate equilibrium. What was dust last year may be water this year, reed marsh the next, then dust once more.

These shifts can be traced through the patterns of vegetation. Whenever the swamp extends itself, fast-growing papyrus is quick to move in and colonise new areas of the *melapo* or floodplain; whereas the tall stands of slow-growing hyphaene palms take longer to establish themselves and are indicators of older inundations.

When the floods are up they divide the delta into a million islands. Many are literally no more than anthills, old termite mounds small enough to be encompassed by the shade of a single palm tree. Others, like Chief's Island, named after Chief Moremi of the Batswana people, who created the Moremi Wildlife Reserve, are bigger than New York and home to a host of animals: leopard and lion, large herds of elephant and thunderous cavalcades of buffalo.

Shinde Island, buried so deep in the papyrus that it takes a forty-five minute trip from Xugana to reach it, is a perfect microcosm of the Okavango, a self-contained lost world in miniature, complete with its own plains, swamps and acacia groves. The camp on Shinde, like the one at Pom-Pom, is run in grand style by Ker and Downey, an offshoot of the Nairobi-based safari company with offices in Maun. Like all their camps, it is small but luxurious, with just seven twin-bedded tents, an open-air dining room and a circle of chairs set around a campfire under a tall ebony tree.

I had come to Shinde with David Coulson, the photographer who had accompanied me on my journey through Namibia. David was an old friend from Kenya, where we had travelled widely together; but we had never been on safari in Botswana. A fair-haired, big-boned Englishman (in Nairobi he is known as *Bwana Mrefu* — Mister Tall), he was born in Paris, the son of a British diplomat. Having completed his education in England he embarked upon a careeer in management consultancy; but in 1980 he threw it up to follow his star to Africa, where he has lived ever since, looking at its wildlife and wild places through the lens of his camera.

One morning at Shinde we set out early to look for Shaka Zulu, a magnificent, twelve-year-old black-maned lion with a missing tail-tuft, whose resident pride of eight lionesses had just produced two litters of tiny cubs. We had heard him roaring as the sun was rising, and soon found his broad pugmarks leading down a dusty trail only a mile from camp.

The air was crisp and clean and dry, filled with the hay-meadow smell of Africa. The low light flooded across the plains, picking out a trio of giraffes in sharp relief as they strode along the horizon. Moments later we came upon a lechwe staring nervously into the long grass; and there was Shaka, no more than twenty yards away; a silent, tawny shadow, padding through the dawn on his big soft paws.

He sniffed the breeze as he walked, heading purposefully towards an anthill.

Then suddenly he bounded towards it and began to dig furiously, throwing great clouds of dirt between his back legs like a dog searching for a bone. A warthog had made its den in the side of the anthill and Shaka was trying to drag it out. For half an hour he clawed and burrowed, his powerful shoulders bunching with effort as he tried to seize the terrified pig. From time to time he would pause and back out of the hole to stare at us with stony eyes, then shake the dust from his tousled mane and begin again. But the den proved too deep, and in the end he wandered off to seek the shade.

There were more lions at Machaba, another of Ker and Downey's delta camps, set at the edge of the Khwai River, which trickles through the dense reeds and tall yellow grasses in a chain of lilyponds and hippo pools. The camp takes its name from the machaba trees — the sycamore figs whose mottled trunks and generous shade protect the tents from the heat of the day. It is a wonderful spot to sit and watch elephant and kudu coming out of the woods to drink; and there is always a good chance of seeing lions.

At Machaba we found fresh lion tracks within minutes of leaving camp. There were two sets of prints — a lion and lioness, said Willie Senkora, our Motswana driver-guide. Willie used to be a waiter but always dreamed of becoming a safari guide. Now, dressed in jungle-green bush fatigues, he is an expert at reading sign and finding game.

Sure enough, we caught up with the lions not far away, walking across a plain of bleached blond grass. We approached slowly, keeping a respectful distance. Even so, the male turned for no apparent reason and bared his canines. Then his tail began to thrash irritably — always a bad sign.

When he came for us, covering the ground in great galloping bounds, Willie was ready. He gunned the engine and our open-topped Toyota Land-Cruiser pulled swiftly away from the charging cat. I was hugely relieved, but David Coulson, hanging out of the back with his camera at the ready, was plainly unhappy. 'Couldn't we stop for just one more picture?' he pleaded.

'You know, in all my time in the bush that was the first time I have ever been charged by a lion,' said Willie afterwards.

'Me too, Willie,' I told him.

It was an extraordinary incident. It served to demonstrate both the unpredictability of wild animals and the need always to treat the 'big five' — lion, leopard, elephant, buffalo and black rhino — with the utmost respect. Willie's driving had been beyond reproach. He had shown concern for the safety of his clients and had been at great pains not to disturb the lions by driving too close. Yet still the male had been provoked into a charge.

As with the leopard which had charged my vehicle in the Luangwa Valley, it had happened so fast there was no time to be afraid. Being pursued by an irate elephant was far more terrifying, and being chased on foot by a hippo in the Masai Mara was certainly the closest I have ever come to being killed. But these moments of high drama always nagged at my conscience. The ideal way to watch animals, I felt, was to be an invisible observer, to intrude as little as possible into their world. Only then was it possible to see natural behaviour.

Mercifully, perhaps, our encounter with the lions provided the only surge of adrenalin in an otherwise indolent world. What I remember most about Machaba is its drowsy warmth and delicious sense of languorous calm. After lunch, lulled by the hypnotic calls of barbets and hornbills and sad-voiced wood doves, I would lie in my tent until the call came to afternoon tea, followed by one last game drive before sundown.

At night the breeze rustled the dried seedpods of the rain trees with a soothing sound. The moon rose. Bell frogs chimed in the darkness and the tinder-dry mopane logs glowed red in the open hearth. Overhead Centaurus and the Southern Cross glittered like diadems and Lupus, the constellation of the wolf, hunted in a forest of stars.

Sometimes, waking in the small hours when even the frogs had fallen silent, I would hear elephants shaking down showers of acacia pods behind the camp kitchen; and once, from somewhere across the river, the deep-throated grunts of a lion, fading, fading.

Every morning I rose before the sun, to be greeted by francolins calling and the sweet song of a Heuglin's robin. Despite the cold and the earliness of the hour I could not wait to be out in the bush again. The air smelled of dust and grass and game, laced with the spicy pungence of camphor bush and wild African sage crushed under our wheels.

At such times, gazing at the immense horizons, the endless vistas of waving grass, the blue walls of faraway forests, it was impossible not to be profoundly moved by the heady sense of space and freedom, to rediscover Africa's lost age of innocence, to share the world of lions and antelope and to feel one's spirit rushing forward across the plains like the flights of doves that hurtled past on their way to water.

Every drive brought fresh surprises to delight the senses. One day it was the sight of a majestic kudu bull with chalk-striped flanks and spiral horns, walking down to drink at a pool. The next, a family of ground hornbills, ungainly birds the size of turkeys, with scarlet wattles and black plumage, slow-marching through the grass like a funeral procession. They called as they walked, their sombre, booming voices carrying for miles across the surrounding bush, claiming sovereignty over their territory.

Inevitably, it is the elephants that make the greatest impression. Their very size commands respect, and Botswana's elephants are both larger and more numerous than most, the bulls carrying thick, heavy ivory of a kind no longer seen in East Africa since the poaching holocaust of the 1980s.

One of the best places to see them is in the Moremi, the wildlife reserve which preserves 6,430 square miles of the delta between the Khwai and Boro Rivers. Extending deep into the swamps from Chobe National Park to Chief's

Island, it is named after Chief Moremi of the Batawana people and was the first big-game sanctuary in southern Africa to be established by an African tribe on their own land. Today it is renowned not only for elephants but also as a sanctuary for two of Africa's most endangered mammals — the roan antelope and the wild dog. Roan are seen regularly along now the Khwai River floodplains, and the Moremi's wild dog packs now represent about 30 per cent of the entire African population.

Elephants love the Moremi's woodlands. Even when you cannot see them you know they are there, tearing down the mopane trees with cracks like gunshots. Their presence is everywhere. Their stableyard smell hangs in the air; their giant footprints flatten the dust. And sometimes, from the depths of the forests, their strident trumpetings split the silence.

In the midst of this vast kingdom of elephants, on Pom-Pom Island, is Abu's Camp, springboard for the ultimate safari. Abu is an African elephant bull, a magnificent ten-foot, thirty-year-old tusker, and for five unforgettable days I rode on his broad back, swaying and splashing across the drowned floodplains on a slow march through paradise.

There is a long-held belief that African elephants, unlike their Asian cousins, are treacherous, unpredictable and untrainable. But Randall Jay Moore, an American biologist, Vietnam war protester and animal trainer, has turned conventional wisdom on its head by offering elephant-riding safaris in Botswana.

His three adult elephants, Abu, Benny and Cathy, were reintroduced to Africa from circus and zoo life in America, where they had originally been sent as orphans. Now they, in turn, have adopted seven baby elephants, survivors of a cull in Kruger National Park.

Abu, Randall's pride and joy, who can respond to seventy commands, has starred in several films, including *White Hunter, Black Heart*, in which he appeared with Clint Eastwood; but it is as a riding elephant that he excels.

Padding soundlessly through the mopane woodlands, splashing belly-deep across lily-covered lagoons, Abu is in his element, a perfect six-ton, all, purpose vehicle of awesome power, eco-friendly and, apart from a few cavernous rumblings at the rear, entirely pollution-free.

I soon discovered that lounging in a padded howdah is not only as comfortable as an armchair, it is also the ideal vantage point from which to view the Okavango. Often, when travelling by *mokoro*, you are enclosed by towering walls of reeds; but on elephant-back ten feet above the ground, you can see everything.

Every morning I would meet the elephants behind the camp. There, at the command 'Stretch down', Abu, Benny and Cathy would lower their giant bodies and allow us to climb aboard. Then, to Randall's cry of 'Come, babies, come', we would ride out through the reeds with the seven small elephants hurrying trunk-to-tail in our wake.

For the elephants our daily excursions were one long, movable feast, a steady procession from one succulent mouthful of palm fronds or mopane leaves to the next. For me, after twenty years of travelling across Africa, this was the greatest adventure of them all.

Ours was a true journey into the wilderness. Freed from the tyranny of roads and vehicles, we could go where we pleased, wandering among cool glades of mopane and ebony trees, following hippo trails through silver-tasselled reeds even taller than ourselves, eating up the ground at a steady three miles per hour. And always there were animals to look at: a leopard in a leadwood tree; three old buffalo bulls with massive horns'; herds of lechwe splashing away through the shallows.

One magical morning we strode right into a pack of fourteen wild dogs resting at the water's edge. After their initial surprise, they appeared quite unconcerned. Even though the alpha female was heavily pregnant, she allowed us to remain with them for more than an hour near the den where the puppies would soon be born.

One day I joined Randall and walked on foot among the elephants. Hemmed in by a forest of pillared legs, swaying trunks and huge, flapping ears, I listened to their contented rumblings and wondered what it might feel like to be an elephant, part of a family bound by ties of kinship every bit as close as a human's.

Back in camp with the sun going down there would be hot showers as the first reed frogs began to call. Then Lothar Swoboda, the finest chef in the delta, would conjure up a magnificent dish of fresh-caught bream or Botswana beef, followed by coffee around the campfire.

Lothar had a friend, a glamorous redhead called Valentina, whom I met one morning. Softly she nibbled my ear while I shaved outside my tent. Valentina was a tame fishing owl, a magnificent creature with rich orange feathers, who had hatched on St Valentine's Day. Fishing owls are rare birds and the Okavango is their stronghold.

On my last morning I was treated to an awesome demonstration of the various skills (never tricks, Randall insists) learnt by the elephants for their roles as film stars. At a given command I raised my camera to witness a full-blooded charge from Abu. Through the lens I watched him, a huge and terrifying shadow bearing down on me at full speed. Only when he pulled up in a cloud of dust only yards away did remember Iain Douglas-Hamilton's comment about an elephant charge: 'It's meant to be impressive; elephants have spent millions of years perfecting it.'

Long after I had left Abu's Camp and flown up to the Chobe National Park, the pleasures of those past five days replayed in my mind like an endless video. I remembered the sound of doves in the trees behind my tent, the scent of wild sage crushed underfoot, the bream rising at sunset in the limpid lagoons. I thought about Randall and his ever-present cigar, his rifle and his pony-tail and his wry sense of humour. I thought about the endless cheerfulness of David, my mahout, and Valentina nibbling my ear; but most of all I thought about the elephants: Abu, Benny, Cathy and the babies. Already I missed them more than I could say.

There were more elephants along the Chobe River as I flew into Kasane, but these were wild ones. Even before we landed I could see then, standing out like smooth, dark boulders on the floodplains. Others were emerging from the autumn-coloured woodlands to drink and wallow, and as we circled for our final approach I could see still more emerging from the trees in a golden haze of dust.

Chobe is classic elephant country. It has plenty of trees, abundant water, seemingly limitless space and, apart from tourists in Toyota Land-Cruisers, no people. It is the finest national park in Botswana: 4,000 square miles of pristine wilderness filled with fathomless woodlands of mopane, teak and knobthorn acacias, stretching south from the Chobe River to encompass the tall grasslands of the Mababe Depression, where the big lion prides roam, and westward to the great Linyanti Swamp, with its slumbering hippos and shy sitatunga antelope.

Towards October, in the dry season, the banks of the Chobe River boast the heaviest concentration of elephants on earth, with up to thirteen jumbos for every square mile of parkland. But in November, at the first sign of rain, when the pans and waterholes fill in the interior of the park, they disperse into the boundless woodlands until the dry season returns in May.

There is a lodge at Chobe, called Chobe Chilwero, which is the perfect introduction to life in the Botswana bush. Its name means 'the beholden view', and from the verandah you can look out across the shining river and watch fish eagles circling over the floodplains and the Caprivi Strip beyond.

From Chobe Chilwero, wide roads of soft Kalahari sand lead into the park, passing the large and luxurious Chobe Lodge, where Elizabeth Taylor once honeymooned with Richard Burton. No sooner had we entered the park gate than we found tracks where a herd of sable had crossed just ahead of us; but these beautiful antelope remained elusive, almost mythical creatures, and we glimpsed them only from a distance as they wandered through thick bush on a far hillside, led by a magnificent, midnight-black bull whose scimitar horns curved way back across his powerful shoulders.

But the elephants were everywhere, the sand pressed flat into huge, fresh prints leading to and from the river, and from deeper in the shattered woodlands came the familiar, growling belly-rumbles and the sudden crack of breaking branches where the herds were feeding.

At last we emerged beside the river and watched a solitary bull elephant far out on the floodplain on the opposite bank, rolling towards us through the yellowed grass with his enormous ears spread wide, like an old-time sailing barge running before the wind.

The sun passed down and the sky turned orange as more elephants strode out of the trees, drifting soundlessly through a haze of dust that hung and glowed in the dying light. Long after the sun had set, the sky still smouldered like the going down of a great fire, the river aflame and the silhouettes of the elephants, motionless now, rooted to their reflections along the shore, at peace with their world as flight upon flight of white-faced ducks fled from the night to their roost in the west, filling the sky with their whistling cries.

This is the spectacle that two decades of slaughter by ivory poachers has largely destroyed elsewhere in Africa. Yet it still survives in Chobe, where a fortunate combination of chance and benign neglect has left Botswana with the largest secure elephant population on the continent. In this respect Botswana is the very opposite of Kenya, whose 20,000 elephants are now virtually marooned within the national parks by one of the fastest-growing human populations in the world. While the poaching holocaust raged across the west of Africa, Botswana's elephants remained insulated by a fluke of geography. To the south lies the security-conscious Republic of South Africa, where political tensions kept the border tightly patrolled, making it difficult for poachers to operate. To the west lie the deserts of Namibia, until recently also patrolled by the South Africans, as was the Caprivi Strip to the north. That left Zimbabwe, on Botswana's north-eastern border, which not only has thousands of elephants of its own, but also operates a strict shoot-to-kill policy against poachers.

As a result, Botswana — formerly the British protection of Bechuanaland — is one of the very few countries whose elephant population has increased. Nobody knows exactly how many elephants there are, especially as herds migrate back and forth across the Zimbabwean border. The best estimates put the figure at around 60,000, and so far, unlike Zimbabwe and South Africa, there has been no culling of excess numbers.

That Botswana can afford the luxury of so many elephants is another stroke of good fortune. Although the country is roughly the size of France it has fewer than one and a quarter million people. Much of the land is dominated by the flat and arid Kalahari Desert; but the economy is stable, underpinned by the world's richest diamond mines. With one fifth of the land occupied by 80 per cent of its people, Botswana is one of the last places on earth where large numbers of elephants can still set out on their long journeys without coming into serious conflict with humanity.

That evening, back at Chobe Chilwero, I sat by the campfire with André Martens, the lodge's resident guide and naturalist. Lean and tanned by long years in the bush, he wore a leather Crocodile Dundee hat and sat warming his hands over the glowing embers. His family has been in Africa since 1705,

Top: A mother elephant and her calf. Elephants are highly social animals bound by close ties of kinship which may last a lifetime. *(Jonathan Scott)*

Bottom: The most intimate way to explore the Okavango is to be poled along in a *mokoro* – the traditional delta dugout canoe. *(David Coulson)*

Top: Gareth Patterson with a lion's skull. 'I have wept many tears for the lions of Africa, and will no doubt weep many more.' *(Gareth Patterson)*

Bottom: George Adamson celebrating his 83rd birthday at Kora with lion cub and champagne. *(David Coulson)*

Top: The old man and his heir apparent: George Adamson with Gareth Patterson at Kora in 1989. *(Gareth Patterson)*

Bottom: Londolozi leopard. Nowhere else in Africa offers such regular close-ups of this elusive predator. *(Brian Jackman)*

Gareth Patterson with Furaha, one of the last of the *Born Free* lionesses. *(Gareth Patterson)*

he told me. We drank beer and talked long into the night about the plight of the African elephant and the shortcomings of CITES, which had tried to control the ivory haemorrhage by imposing a system of quotas and permits, but had failed utterly to staunch the illegal flow of tusks leaving Africa.

Only in the more politically stable south, in Zimbabwe, Botswana and South Africa, were the elephants spared the worst excesses of the ivory slaughter. In addition, although big-game hunting for lions, buffaloes and other trophy animals still flourishes in Botswana, elephant-hunting had been banned in 1983. Since then, Botswana's elephants have been allowed to come and go in peace. But if they continue to multiply, the pressures to control their numbers may become irresistible.

The question — to cull or not to cull — has dominated and divided conservation power politics in Africa for years. In one camp are the southern African states and their supporters in the ivory trade, who favour culling in their unsentimental pursuit of sustainable utilisation as the best way to manage their wildlife resources. In other words, wildlife must have an economic value if it is to survive in Africa today. Their pragmatic approach to conservation is simple, and can best be summed up in a single phrase: if it pays, it stays.

In Zimbabwe and South Africa, where culls have been regularly carried out in the past, profits from the sale of meat, skins and tusks are ploughed back into park management or used to benefit the local people, who sometimes suffer the depredations of crop-raiding elephants. Such policies have worked well in these countries, where there is less corruption and parks and reserves are effectively patrolled. Understandably, they want to go on selling their ivory and are therefore in favour of a managed ivory trade.

Opposing them is the rest of Africa, led by Kenya and Tanzania and backed by the European Community and the United States, who had been major consumers of ivory prior to the trade ban in 1989. They do not oppose the necessity of culling. They simply argued that nothing short of an international moratorium on ivory trading would halt the elephants' headlong rush to extinction.

Those advocating a cull in Botswana include scientists and conservationists who are genuinely concerned about the destruction of Chobe's riverine woodlands; but the fiercest lobbying has come from the ivory trade and its supporters in Zimbabwe. The controversy has left Botswana's conservation movement hopelessly divided. Most people in Gaborone, the capital, favoured a cull; but in Chobe and the Okavango Delta, where the elephants are a major tourist attraction, bringing 30,000 visitors a year, local people and tour operators alike remain bitterly opposed to it.

There is a cruel paradox here. When elephants are properly protected they multiply to the point where the habitat begins to collapse under the sheer weight of numbers. When this happens there is at present no alternative to culling. But in Botswana, the defenders of the elephants say there is no evidence that the critical point has been reached.

André Martens is a pragmatist. He was in favour of culling and supported the theory of sustainable utilisation. That was how it was done in South Africa and Zimbabwe, and even in Botswana, he believed, a cull was the only way to keep the herds in check.

Yet he was no bloodthirsty killer. 'Listen, man,' he said in his quiet South African voice with its flat, clipped vowels. 'I've culled ellies and believe me, it's no fun. You have to take out whole families, because the little ones can't survive without their mothers.' Once, after he had shot a cow elephant during a culling operation, her baby calf had run towards him, trying to chase him away. 'And I knew that it, too, would have to be shot,' he said. 'But I couldn't do it, man. I had tears in my eyes and I gave my gun to my African tracker and told him to shoot.'

I argued the view put forward by Richard Leakey, that to allow even a limited resumption of the ivory trade would be disastrous. Even the legitimate sale of ivory derived from culling would be enough to prop up the price, sustain the demand and provide a smokescreen which the old, evil triumvirate of poachers, corrupt middlemen and traders would flourish as before. But Martens was not to be shaken from his beliefs.

Our talk left me in a sombre mood; but next morning the sun shone from a sky of faultless blue and it was impossible not to be in high spirits as I set off early before breakfast, heading for the river. André kept a small outboard motor there, and had promised to show me a party trick he had perfected during his time at Chobe.

We cast off and idled downstream. The river was like a mirror. Pied kingfishers hovered overhead and large monitor lizards with speckled gold skins sunned themselves at the water's edge. André carried with him a plastic bag of silver bream he had caught the previous day. Now he cut a length of papyrus reed stem and inserted it into one end of the fish. The reed had the buoyancy of cork and would prevent it from sinking.

At last we were ready. André tossed the bream into the water, no more than a boat's length away. He cupped his hands to his lips and the cry of the fish eagle flew from his throat.

An eagle had been watching us from a dead tree nearby. Now, at the sound of André's voice, it launched itself towards us on broad black and chestnut wings. It came in low with a rush of air. Then, with perfect timing, it thrust forward its crooked yellow fists to scoop up the fish and return to its perch.

Like the Okavango, the waters of the Chobe River are born in the highlands of Angola. From there they come swirling down the Kwando River to lose themselves in the Linyanti Swamp, the whispering wilderness of papyrus beds and winding channels that form the north-west frontier of the Chobe Park. Eventually the Kwando re-emerges from the marshes, but with a new identity, first as the Linyanti River and then in its final metamorphosis as the Chobe, a tributary of the mighty Zambezi.

In June and July, when the floods spread through the Linyanti Swamp, the waters spread out and replenish the Selinda Spillway, linking these northern wetlands with the Okavango Delta. Selinda lies outside the park, but the presence of the spillway attracts heavy concentrations of game in the dry season: elephants, buffaloes, zebras, wildebeest, impala and giraffes, as well as all the major predators.

Selinda is a hunting concession area, but a small bush camp had been set up there for photographic safaris, with accommodation for half a dozen clients and a dining tent perched on the flattened top of an old termite mound at the edge of the spillway.

When I was there last the camp was run by Mike Penman, a bearded, barrel-chested South African whose greatest passion in life was tracking lions. He had learned his bushcraft from a Shangaan tracker at the Londolozi Game Reserve in South Africa, and could read spoor like a man perusing the morning paper. 'It's all there in the dust if you can understand it,' he said. 'Spoor is like a tape cassette of everything that has happened in the last twenty-four hours with only the sound missing.'

He jabbed a finger at the maze of fresh prints which had blossomed on the game trails overnight. Here a zebra had rolled; there a hyena had crossed the road. 'And here,' he said, pointing to a line of broad, four-toed pugmarks, 'are fresh lion tracks.'

We followed their trail across an open plain where the coarse yellow grass had been grazed to stubble, and came to a shallow stream. As we drove along its banks, looking for the place where the lions might have crossed, blacksmith plovers rose at our approach and flights of doves hurtled over our heads as they came in from the mopane woodlands to drink and bathe.

Eventually we caught up with them, a big grey lioness and a young male, a nervous two-year-old with the makings of a splendid mane. Mike knew them both. They belonged to a pride of five lionesses whose only adult pride male had been shot not long ago by trophy hunters. Mike was as tough as teak, but behind his slightly forbidding exterior lurked a gentle soul with a quiet voice, and he worried constantly that the same fate might soon befall the two-year-old, which had become his favourite lion. Even as we watched, we became aware that we ourselves were being observed by a group of hunters in the distant trees.

Later, after we had driven away, three shots rang out, casting a shadow over the rest of the day. We never saw the sub-adult lion again, although Mike was sure he had found his tracks, still accompanied by those of the old grey lioness. I, too, hoped the hunters hadn't shot him, and I like to think of him as I last saw him, standing on a termite mound with the wind lifting the hackles of his mane as he stared across the floodplain.

Even in camp there was life to observe. In a tree near my tent lived a sparrowhawk which dashed out to catch small birds and brought them back to pluck and eat on an overhanging branch. A chameleon resided outside the camp kitchen, green as the bush to which it clung; and once, dozing on my bed after lunch, I woke to see a slender mongoose peering into my tent; a lithe, brown creature, weasel-thin, with delicate whiskers and a black tail-tip.

My tent was half-hidden in a leafy thicket whose shade I shared with a swamp boubou, a skulking black and white shrike with a blood-red eye and the strangest call, which began with a frog-like croak but then broke into a pure, flute-like whistle. Sometimes, resting on my bed after lunch, it amused me to return his whistles, and we continued these duets for some moments until he was distracted by a passing insect.

The days I spent at Selinda were among the best I had enjoyed in Africa. Partly it was due to Mike Penman's tremendous enthusiasm and his knowledge of the bush; and partly because of the sheer abundance of birds and animals. We saw cheetahs and leopards, beautiful crimson-chested bush shrikes and a six-foot-long black mamba with its unmistakable coffin-shaped head. But whenever I think of Selinda the most powerful image that comes to mind is of the three old elephant bulls who allowed us to approach so close as they rested in the shade of an isolated palm grove.

They were tall and heavy, with broken tusks and ragged ears, and each one must have been at least fifty years old. Locked in their sunken and wise-seeming heads were memories drawn from over half a century of wanderings. They knew the elephant paths their parents had travelled long ago, and where to find water when the land ached with drought, and the secret places in the woodlands where their favourite fruits and seedpods grew.

Farther north, across the Zambezi in Zambia and all the way on up through East Africa into Sudan and Somalia, and westward through the rainforests of the Congo River basin, the big tuskers and the proud old matriarchs had largely disappeared. When the ivory-poaching boom had taken off, they had been the first to fall, and with them had gone their precious knowledge, the entire culture of a species, leaving the structure of the remaining herds in chaos.

That is why, like Richard Leakey, I believe that a permanent ivory trade ban is the only way to secure the survival of the African elephant throughout most of its range and allow time for the shell-shocked herds to recover. The alternative is a resumption of the ivory war which has already cost hundreds of human lives, leading in perhaps as little as ten years to the unthinkable tragedy of a world without elephants.

Today Botswana stands at the crossroads. Although it seems as if a pilot culling programme may go ahead, the government may yet draw back from going down the same road as Zimbabwe. If so, Botswana will retain its unique position as the last true kingdom of the elephant.

In Botswana one can still enjoy the sight of elephant families wandering undisturbed through the bush with a degree of protection that has allowed them to reach their full span and attain the huge size and heavy tusks of the animals I saw everywhere in Chobe and the Moremi. Only in Botswana can one approach herd after herd and sense their trust — a trust that will be shattered if the marksmen are invited in.

For the moment it is still possible to rise at dawn and hear the song of the lions, to drive out into the cold, bright African mornings, to live in the sun and the wind and share these last great empty spaces with the elephants. But for how much longer? To live among these wandering giants is to breathe the air of a vanishing freedom and to understand why the world needs elephants if we ourselves are to survive.

Chapter Fourteen
The Last of the Free

George Adamson's death in 1989 was a milestone in the history of Kenya. In his long life he had seen the country come of age, emerging from British colonial rule and the dark days of the Mau Mau campaign to gain full independence under its first President, M'zee Jomo Kenyatta. Under President Moi, Kenyatta's successor, George watched the country settling down, its old frontier spirit fading away as mass tourism pushed ever deeper into the hills and game parks and along the once-deserted shores of the Indian Ocean.

Sadly he never lived to see the end of the ivory trade and the demise of the *shifta*. After George's murder, Richard Leakey's tough new anti-poaching field force swept through northern Kenya, flushing out the Somalis in a series of fierce and bloody skirmishes. By now, too, thanks to the international ivory trade ban, the price at which tusks changed hands in Mogadishu, the Somali capital, had fallen through the floor, from $13.50 per kilo to no more than $1.35. For the poachers the rewards were no longer worth the risks, and the elephants came back from the brink.

From time to time, news filtered down from Kora. According to Dougie Collins, another wonderful old warrior of the same vintage as George, one of the Kora lions had been seen lying on Adamson's grave, just as Karen Blixen had described in *Out of Africa*, when a lion was seen resting on the grave of Denys Finch-Hatton in the Ngong Hills. (Later reports were not so good. In November 1992 I heard that the Somalis had ransacked what was left of George's camp. They desecrated his grave, smashing the headstone into twelve pieces, and set fire to the beautiful riverine forest that grew along the banks of the Tana River.)

As for Batian, Rafiki and Furaha, the three lion cubs George had been looking after at the time he was murdered, I heard that they had been taken down to Botswana by Gareth Patterson, a young Englishman who had volunteered to look after them and, in time, return them to the wild.

One day in 1992 I received an invitation to return to Botswana, to visit Mashatu, a luxury safari lodge in the Tuli Game Reserve. I knew that Gareth and the cubs were living somewhere in the Tuli, which lies at the eastern toe-end of Botswana, wedged between Zimbabwe and the arid low veld of the northern Transvaal. Intrigued to know what had become of George's last lions, I managed to track down an address for Gareth and wrote to him.

A few weeks later a letter arrived out of the blue with a Botswana postmark. Eagerly I tore it open. It was from Gareth. Life at his camp was fairly basic, he warned; but if I didn't mind roughing it for a few days I was most welcome to meet him and his lions.

It was an opportunity too good to miss; and in July I flew down to Johannesburg's Jan Smuts Airport to pick up the local Air Botswana flight to Mashatu.

'Come on, Rafiki; come on, Furaha.' The cry of the young man with the shoulder-length hair carried far in the cold air of a Botswana winter's dawn. Again he cupped his hands to his lips and called, his voice echoing among the stony hills. Silence; and then, from maybe a mile off, the answering *aaounhh* of a lion. His face broke into a grin of pure delight. 'They're coming,' he said.

We waited as the sun came up, flooding the mopane trees with golden light. Suddenly, impala began to snort in alarm. Gareth gestured to me to keep out of sight, afraid that my presence would scare the lions away; then he opened the gate of his camp compound and stepped outside.

Moments later Rafiki appeared, a full-grown lioness in her prime. I could hear the thud of her feet as she ran straight at Gareth, then rose on her hind legs to place her huge front paws over his shoulders, while he in turn hugged her and stroked her tawny flanks. 'Rafiki,' he murmured, and the big lioness grunted with pleasure at seeing her friend again.

This was Rafiki's first visit to the camp for three weeks. She and her sister Furaha were truly independent now, free to come and go as they pleased, and Furaha had two wild-born cubs of her own. Gareth's task was over, but he could not let go. 'You know,' he said, 'whenever they don't turn up I still worry about them as if they were my own daughters.'

Later, when Rafiki and Gareth had finished greeting each other, Furaha appeared, leading her two cubs to drink from the tub of water that Gareth always put out for them. Apart from the water there was no longer any need for the lions to visit him; but still they came when he called, as if they, too, were reluctant to sever the bonds which had held them so close.

Afterwards the lionesses lay side by side in the morning sunlight while the cubs romped and sparred together. They were now a year old. Soon they would lose their milk teeth, to be replaced by the powerful canines that would mark their transition from cubs to sub-adults.

Twelve years ago I had watched George Adamson being greeted in exactly the same way when he introduced me to his wild pride at Kora. It was a sight I had never expected to see again; yet here I was in Botswana, watching the man who had so modestly assumed the Adamson mantle.

With George's death, Rafiki, Furaha and Batian their brother had been orphaned for a second time. Short of a miracle, they would be condemned to a life behind bars in some foreign zoo.

At this point Patterson arrived. Like Adamson, whom he had met for the first time only six months earlier, he believed in the unassailable dignity of wild lions. He could not bear the thought of a lion that was not free, and offered to take the cubs down to Botswana. The Kenyan authorities, glad to get the cubs off their hands, agreed, and in November 1989 Rafiki, Furaha and Batian set out to begin their new life 1,200 miles away in the Tuli Reserve.

When Gareth flew back to Kenya to collect the cubs he was amazed at how much they had grown since he had last seen them. 'They stared at me at first, as if puzzled,' he said. 'Then to my delight they greeted me like a long-lost friend. They had not forgotten.'

Their departure was a memorable day for Patterson, but one tinged with great sadness. As he was placing the tranquillised cubs into the crates for their long journey south, he looked up and saw Abdi, Adamson's old assistant, in tears. Adamson was gone. Now the cubs were going, too.

The similarity between Patterson and Adamson was striking. Lean and sun-tanned, dressed in a faded pair of shorts and sandals, Gareth lacked only the beard and, at twenty eight, the years to be a spitting image of the old man.

He was born in Margate, but apart from two years at school in England, which he hated, he grew up in Malawi. On his eleventh birthday his mother gave him a book which would change his life. It was *Bwana Game*, by George Adamson.

Eight years later, in 1989, he met Adamson in northern Kenya; but long before then he had entered the savage world of the lion, working first as an assistant ranger and then as a safari guide in the Tuli Reserve, where he spent three and a half years getting to know the Tuli lions. 'By then,' says Patterson, 'I'd become totally hooked on lions.'

'Perhaps no other African animal has lost so much range as the lion,' says Patterson, who is as softly spoken as was George was. 'Even ten years ago there were thought to be 200,000. Today there may be no more than 30,000, and everywhere they are losing ground.'

The Tuli lions were a classic example. There were fewer than thirty — all that was left of a population which once roamed right across the northern Transvaal, eastern Botswana and deep into Zimbabwe until hunters, poachers and cattle ranchers took over their kingdom. Today their nearest neighbours live in South Africa's Kruger Park, 200 miles as the lion walks.

The cubs' new home in the Tuli was not unlike Kora: 270 square miles thorn thickets, sand rivers and red rocky hills. It was harsh and dry but also beautiful, and it held plenty of game.

Even before their arrival in Botswana the three young lions, had already learned how to kill guineafowl. But for the next six months Gareth had to teach them how to hunt bigger game. So every day, for up to twelve hours at a time, he led them through the bush, reintroducing them to their inheritance. For their own safety he taught them to shun man and to hide at the first sound

The martial eagle, the largest African eagle, has a wingspan of two metres and can kill small antelopes.
(Jonathan Scott)

Top: The painted wolves of Africa. Wild dogs were once common in the Serengeti. Now Botswana is the best place to see them. *(Jonathan Scott)*

Bottom: Sleeping leopard. Even in repose these beautiful cats have a presence unmatched by any other African predator. *(Jonathan Scott)*

of a vehicle. Above all he gave them security. 'I was their lioness,' he says. 'They were born with the hunting instinct; all I had to do was polish it.'

After that first six months they were truly free. By then, hunting at night, they had learned to kill kudu, warthogs, impala, wildebeest, even a one-ton eland — Africa's biggest antelope. 'The lions seemed so pleased with themselves in those early days,' says Gareth. 'They would return to camp and lead me to their kills as if to say, look how clever we are.'

Patterson's success at establishing the Adamson lions in their new home should have been a cause for celebration; yet he ran into bitter opposition from the scientific establishment. They dismissed his project as 'George Adamson razzmatazz', saying his work was rooted in sentimentality and lacked scientific credibility. The Cat Specialist Group, an offshoot of the International Union for the Conservation of Nature, even suggested in their July 1991 newsletter that his lions should be neutered to maintain the purity of the local lion stock.

Gareth was understandably upset. 'Maybe it would be better if people who make these rash statements should themselves be neutered,' he suggested. 'They rush to judgement with little understanding of the Tuli lions, which are an island population, reduced to inbreeding and developed from only a handful of survivors. I believe the introduction of new blood from Kenya can only be of benefit.'

Of the three Adamson lions, Gareth always had a soft spot for Batian. 'It was a hell of a thing, walking in the bush with Batian, having my hand on his shoulder when he roared at the dawn,' he told me. 'I knew that life would be so much harder for him. As the only male he would have to stand his ground and fight to establish his territory and his pride.'

When he was three years old, Batian got into a fight with two wild male lions who surprised him as he was feeding on a kill. He fought bravely but was badly mauled, one bite severing all but six inches of his tail.

When Gareth found him he was in a bad way. 'He was a long way from camp and too sick to move. So, for the next four nights, I slept by his side to keep away lions and hyenas. He was so trusting. He even allowed me to dig maggots from his neck with my knife.'

Within a month the young lion had made a miraculous recovery — only to be shot dead nine weeks later by a South African farmer. Batian, who had survived for nearly two years in Botswana, lasted just four days in the Transvaal. There, innocent of the fatal mistake he had made by following two lionesses across the border, he paid with his life for the crime of being a lion in the wrong place.

Gareth was devastated by Batian's death. The day after I left him he was due to receive the skin and skull of his beloved lion. It had taken months of pleading and cajoling before the South African authorities finally agreed to return the remains. Now Batian, the orphan who had lived long enough to touch the wild, was coming home. A grave had been dug, a cairn of stones raised to mark the spot where he and Gareth used to sit in the evenings, gazing out across the golden plains.

'I have wept many tears for the lions of Africa,' said Gareth, 'and will no doubt weep many more.' But at least the two lionesses, Rafiki and Furaha, were still alive; and both had given birth when they were three years old — 'the youngest recorded lioness births in the wild,' said Gareth. Rafiki had produced three cubs, and Furaha had twins. Yet there was more heartbreak to come when Rafiki's cubs disappeared after eleven months.

'I feel sure it was a violent death,' said Gareth. One week all three were there. The next week they were gone — almost certainly killed by another wild male.'

A week later Rafiki was on heat again and straight away came looking for Gareth. She still looked on him as the pride male and clearly expected him to do something about it. She made her intentions very plain by presenting herself to him and then urinating all over his T-shirt.

'I felt so sad for her.' he said. 'She had lost her cubs after doing so well. Now she wanted some more. She wouldn't let me back in camp. She just kept rubbing herself against me. And I suddenly realised I was living in two worlds: mine and the lions.'

Shortly before my arrival in the Tuli Reserve, drought had forced Gareth and Julie Davidson, his constant friend for the past three years, to move to a makeshift camp called Tawana — Little Lion. (Gareth himself is known locally as *Ra di Tau* — Mister Lion.)

A trestle bed had been made up for me inside the wire compound, and that night as I lay and looked up at the stars I could hear jackals keening in the cold, and the faraway rumble of a lion, and wondered if it was one of Gareth's pride.

Next morning, before the sun had risen, Gareth had re-lit the camp fire from the previous night's embers and was brewing tea in a soot-blackened kettle.

Tawana was no luxury safari camp. Like George Adamson's old home at Kora, it was a spartan enclosure surrounded by a six-foot wire fence; a zoo turned inside out, with the people inside and the lions on the outside. Home for Gareth and Julie consisted of a couple of sun-bleached tents, a long-drop lavatory with an elephant's jawbone for a seat (an old hunter's trick borrowed from George), and a dining area with hessian sacks for walls and a bare wooden table.

Water is precious in this drought-prone land, and had to be collected in a 40-gallon drum every three days from a spring four miles away. There was no radio. Gareth's only link with the outside world was a battered pick-up truck. 'You don't do this for fun,' he said as we waited for his lions to arrive. 'Who else would live as we do, in a primitive bush camp, worrying about finding sufficient funds to keep going?'

Despite the death of Batian and the loss of Rafiki's cubs, he had struggled on. It had been a gruelling three years, but the magic of living with his lions had never palled. He had achieved what he had set out to do, and it was reward enough to see Rafiki and Furaha and the cubs living wild in the reserve they now claimed as their own.

Then, three months after I had returned to England, tragedy struck the Tuli reserve and shattered Gareth's world forever. On 29 October an African tracker living at a bush camp in the reserve went out at night to relieve himself in the bushes and was fatally mauled by a lion.

Next morning Furaha and her two fifteen-month-old cubs were found nearby, and were destroyed by Botswana Wildlife Department rangers, leaving Rafiki as the sole surviving Adamson lion.

Fortunately for Rafiki she was several miles away at the time, feasting on an eland she had killed near Gareth's camp. But now she and Gareth had been given their marching orders by the reserve's owners. 'I'm devastated,' he told me. 'I feel greatly for the dead man's family and I mourn the loss of my lions.'

Inevitably, the incident provoked the same kind of criticism that had been levelled against George Adamson in Kenya, that hand-reared lions lose their fear of man. Patterson strongly disagrees. He believes the victim was attacked simply because he was squatting — a posture known to elicit a threatening response in predators.

'The incident did not occur because Furaha was a lion rehabilitated back into the wild. She had lived as a free lion for two and a half years, during which time she was no more of a threat to people than any other Tuli lion.'

Often, during the time I stayed with Gareth and his lions, I found myself thinking of George Adamson and the days I had spent with him at Kora, and his worries over what would happen to his lions when he was gone.

At least the old man would have found some consolation in knowing that Batian and Furaha both tasted freedom before they were killed. As for Rafiki, she has since given birth to three more cubs; but Botswana's Wildlife Department remained adamant that she must leave the Tuli.

Meanwhile, Gareth Patterson continues to defend Rafiki while trying to find her a new home. 'She will still come to me if I call her,' he says. 'But she will stay away from anyone else. She is scared of people. She is a wild lion now, and poses no greater threat than any other lion in Botswana.'

Chapter Fifteen
The Leopards of Londolozi

Early morning in the Transvaal low-veld, and the South African summer is slipping into autumn. Elephants are feeding under the marula trees, shaking down showers of ripe fruit. Already the European swallows have flown. Soon the impala rut will begin, filling the air with the clack of horns as the males duel for dominance.

Seated in an open-sided Land-Rover, I set out on a dawn game drive, bumping down the sandy trails of the MalaMala Game Reserve. The dew has not yet dried, the air is cool, the sky a faultless blue as we cross a shallow valley where zebras are moving through the scattered thorn thickets, tearing at the grass with black velvet muzzles.

On the far side of the valley we pass a jackal-berry tree, its trunk rubbed smooth by passing game. A fresh set of large, bird-like footprints indicate the recent presence of a rhino. 'Old three-toes has been here in the night,' says Angus Sholto-Douglas, my guide at MalaMala.

These days rhinos are a rare sight in Africa; but here in the north-eastern Transvaal, at the edge of the great Kruger National Park, a visitor would be unlucky not to find them.

The Kruger is by far the biggest national park in South Africa; an area the size of Wales nudging up against the Mozambique border. At the turn of the century, just after its creation, you could have counted Kruger's elephants on the fingers of two hands. Today there are more than 8,000 of them. Along with the rest of the 'big five' (rhino, buffalo, lion and leopard), they are the megastars of a park which supports more wildlife species than any other African game stronghold.

The Kruger, however, is a state-run enterprise, geared to local tourist needs; and most overseas visitors head for the upmarket comforts and greater seclusion of the private reserves on its western boundary. MalaMala is the biggest, covering 45,000 acres, and its main camp on the banks of the Sand River is widely regarded as the world's most luxurious safari lodge.

Despite the 5.30 wake-up calls for the early morning game drives, life at MalaMala follows a relaxing routine. Picnic lunches by the swimming pool; four o'clock tea and cakes on the verandah; then more game-viewing before dinner under the stars in a bamboo *boma*.

'Try the impala wrapped in pastry,' urges Angus Sholto-Douglas, who is definitely not a bunny-hugger. 'It's delicious; Bambi en croute.'

Sholto-Douglas, a thickset young man with rugger-player's legs, is MalaMala's head ranger. Wherever we go he carries a .475 calibre rifle, and gives the impression that if a lion was ever foolish enough to bite him it would not get a second chance.

Next morning we are off into the bush again, Angus at the wheel and Saliot, his Shangaan tracker, perched behind us, wrapped in an old army greatcoat to ward off the dawn chill.

The Shangaan, an offshoot of the Zulu nation, are famous trackers, and this is their country. MalaMala is Shangaan for sable antelope. Ironically, over the next three days, it is the only large mammal we don't see.

We cross the Matshaphiri sand river and find our first leopard. Sholto-Douglas knows her well. She is not long independent of her mother, he tells me, but has proved adept at hunting for herself and is in perfect condition. We leave the track and follow her, ducking under the wicked hooks of the buffalo thorns, flattening the silver-leafed raisin bushes beneath our open Land-Rover until she disappears into a gully.

These low-veld reserves on the edge of the Kruger offer the best leopard-viewing in Africa. The adjoining Londolozi Reserve is generally acknowledged to be the world's best for leopards. But MalaMala must run it a close second, and from time to time offers an additional thrill in the shape of the so-called 'king cheetah'.

These extraordinary animals are not a separate species. They are simply a gorgeous freak of nature, a hiccup in the gene pool which occasionally, produces an animal with a marbled coat instead of spots; and MalaMala is just about the only place in Africa where you might see one.

Over dinner one night, Mike Rattray, MalaMala's owner, told me how Lady Thatcher had seen one in 1991. 'She had unbelievable luck,' he said. 'She actually saw a king cheetah kill. I was there, and before that I'd never even seen a king cheetah myself.'

Rattray also related how the Iron Lady's vehicle was charged by an elephant. 'Everyone else fell to the floor,' he said. 'But Maggie didn't move. She just glared at it, and in the end it turned and went away.'

Sadly, I never saw a king cheetah; but MalaMala did have a special treat in store. On my last morning we found a pack of five wild dogs resting by a river. Sholto-Douglas punched the air with excitement. They were the first he'd seen for eight months.

Wild dogs are Africa's most endangered predators. They are also its most efficient killers, and we had found them, appropriately perhaps, at a spot called the Styx River crossing.

They must have hunted at first light, for their bellies were swollen with meat. Now they rested in the grass, dark shapes with brindled coats, big ears and terrifying teeth.

An hour passed. The sun grew hotter. Doves chanted from the riverside trees and still the dogs slept on.

'I can't believe our luck,' said Sholto-Douglas. 'They range across such enormous distances. They will have moved in from the Kruger. This evening they'll kill again. Tomorrow they could be twenty miles away.'

The summer rains had been kind to Ngala. Now the land was drying out. Already the grass was as yellow as a lion's coat, and it would not be long before the mopane woodlands took on the orange hues of autumn, heralding the cold bright dawns and hot dry days of the South African winter.

At the beginning of the 1980s a game lodge was built here on the western fringes of the Kruger park. Today, in a unique partnership with the state-run Parks Board, the lodge has been taken over by the Conservation Corporation, a South African organisation whose commitment to the well-being of wildlife and local people alike is attracting worldwide recognition.

The Conservation Corporation is an eco-tourism company set up in 1990 by two brothers, Dave and John Varty, owners of Londolozi private game reserve. The Varty brothers believe in the conservation ethic known as sustainable living.

'We have to show that man and wildlife can live together on a sustainable basis,' says Dave Varty. 'It's the only answer. And we can only do it if the local people benefit from our activities. When that happens, as it does at Londolozi, the living standards for everyone involved improve dramatically, and the land and the wildlife are again seen as something worth caring for.'

Clearly the Varty brothers are idealists; but they are also hard-headed businessmen. They know that all over Africa, while cattle farming is failing, the value of marginal land is soaring as its wildlife and tourism potential is being realised. That is why they launched the Conservation Corporation to create wildlife parks throughout southern Africa, using Londolozi as a model.

What the Varty brothers have achieved in breaking down racial barriers would be considered extraordinary anywhere in the world. That they have succeeded in South Africa of all places is truly remarkable, and holds out a ray of hope for this beautiful, long-suffering country. At Ngala, as at Mala Mala, the local people involved are the Shangaan. Ngala is their word for lion. At first they were suspicious when the corporation took over. Now they are enthusiastic supporters, and already the Vartys' enlightened approach has begun to bear fruit.

Discreetly hidden behind the lodge is the village where the African staff and their families live. For the first time in their lives, they now have a clinic with a full-time nurse. There is a soccer pitch, a kindergarten and a village shop run on co-operative lines, with dividends for the villagers. At the same time, new houses with lovingly tended garden plots are replacing the squalid, barrack-like accommodation provided by the former state regime. The new buildings follow the traditional Shangaan style, but hot water is provided by modern, state-of-the art solar-heating panels.

'We don't want a game reserve where the local people are living on the outside, looking through the fence with covetous eyes at the white man's playground,' says Hugh Marshall, Ngala's manager.

For guests, too, the imprint of the new owners is everywhere. The lodge has been elevated into the luxury league. In the evenings, candlelight glitters on crystal glasses and polished silver. The tableware is Villeroy and Boch. Dinner is prepared by a cordon bleu chef.

Next morning, wearing two sweaters for a chilly dawn game drive, I discover another treat. Ngala has its own fleet of open-topped Land-Rovers. There are seven in all and, unlike the Kenyan experience, where vehicles sometimes crowd around lions like Custer's Last Stand, they are the only ones you see.

Justin Carey, my white South African ranger, is a man of impeccable manners, always careful not to stress the animals by driving too fast or too close to them. He and Eric, our Shangaan tracker, work as a team; a partnership built on mutual respect.

When we set off, cruising slowly down a soft sandy trail, I discover another feature of South African safaris. In East Africa, where game country is mostly open savannah, you hunt for game by sight; but in the thick bush of the eastern. Transvaal you find your animals by following tracks.

Perched on the nose of the bonnet, Eric reads the signs in the sand. His skill is uncanny. I have spent enough time in the bush to identify the maze of prints spread out before us: giraffe, zebra, elephant, lion. But Eric can tell if the lion is a male or female, and how long ago it passed this way, and if it was walking, running or stalking.

Ngala is typical of the Kruger low-veld. Like much of Africa it is a sea of bush; flat country, but never dull. Elephants love its dappled woodlands. Lions haunt its thorny thickets. Ahead of us, an African hawk eagle glides over the trees. On either side of the trail we pass golden orb spiders, their giant webs strung like tennis nets between the bushes, tough enough to trap small finches.

The bush is never silent. The air quivers to the hum of insects, to the mindless clucking of yellow-billed hornbills, and the weary song of a small black and white bird called the chinspot batis, whistling its three notes over and over again to the tune of 'Three Blind Mice'.

Farther down the trail we run into a breeding herd of elephants feeding in thick mopane scrub. From all around us comes the sound of branches cracking, slow munchings and noisy defecations. Suddenly they're all around us, no more than a trunk's length away: tiny calves with Dumbo ears, teenage bulls and a dozen huge matriarchs, including one old cow with crossed tusks.

They seem peaceful enough, but a sudden belly rumble brings an instant mood swing. Ears flapping, they begin to trumpet their unease. Then, heads high, tails up, they turn and vanish into the bush.

When we are not watching elephants or looking for lion tracks, Justin regales me with snippets of bush lore. I learn, for example, that a twig from the magic guarri bush makes an ideal toothbrush; that the seed pods of the russet bush willow are as good as any tea-bags; and that an oxpecker can remove up to 1,000 ticks a day from a buffalo's muddy hide.

I spend three days at Ngala and no two game drives are the same. In the afternoons we go out with the sun and come back with the stars. Towards sundown, the wind dies, the light turns to gold. Shadows reach out across the grass and crested francolins begin to call, a repetitive phrase which sounds like 'beer and cognac'.

As if on cue, Justin opens the cool-box. There is a choice of chilled wines and beers. I grab a can of Castle and we sit and wait for the evening star to appear, followed soon after by the Southern Cross, then another and another, until the heavens are ablaze. On our way home, Eric switches on the spotlight and we pick out an aardwolf, a rare, insectivorous hyena. Justin is overjoyed: it's the first he has seen.

On my last morning at Ngala we witness our first kill. Driving along the banks of the Timbavati River we are treated to the ludicrous spectacle of four adult lionesses chasing an African hare. We are so close that I can hear the thump of their paws on the dried-up riverbed.

Five minutes later we round a bend in the river to find a table spread with a white cloth, covered with bowls of fresh fruit and cereals. In no time, Eric is frying eggs and bacon. A wonderful surprise: breakfast in the bush with the lions.

On our way back to the lodge we drive along the boundary which divides Ngala's 54 square miles from the Kruger park. Until recently there was a fence here. Now only rusting posts remain and the animals can roam freely again, following old migration routes denied them for so long.

All down the Kruger's western boundary the fences are coming down, sweeping away the old divisions between state-owned land and private reserves. Their removal is an apt and powerful metaphor for what is happening in South Africa today, where the dismantling of apartheid is encouraging bold new initiatives of the kind taking place at Ngala.

The policies behind the greening of Ngala were pioneered at Londolozi, just ten minutes away by light aircraft. Like Ngala, its 54 square miles lie up against the western edges of the Kruger on the banks of the Sand River.

Londolozi is the Conservation Corporation's flagship, and its lodge is the finest I have ever stayed at. It is also the only game lodge in the world to be included in the Paris-based *Relais et Châteaux* hotel guide.

It is really three lodges in one: Main Camp, Bush Camp with just eight rooms, and Tree Camp, where lunch is served on a balcony suspended 80 feet up in an ancient ebony tree.

Here, secure in my own spacious chalet, I slept soundly between crisp cotton sheets in a king-size bed. Outside was a balcony, shaded by majestic tamboti and jackal-berry trees, looking down on the Sand River. As for the food, the buffet lunches and candlelit suppers were, if anything, even better than at Ngala.

Yet its greatest luxury had nothing to do with cuisine or comfort. What Londolozi uniquely offers are virtually guaranteed sightings of Africa's most elusive big cat, the leopard.

For me, ever since those early days in the Mara with Jonathan Scott, leopards exude a special magic. They are such mysterious creatures, so beautiful and so highly skilled in the arts of concealment that even the briefest glimpse is a delight.

But at Londolozi, thanks to years of patience and dedication on the part of the reserve's rangers and trackers, the leopards have learned to accept the presence of safari vehicles and are now seen on a daily basis.

It all began in 1979 when a leopard known as the Tugwaan Female produced two cubs. It was the first time that anyone had ever seen such small cubs at Londolozi and it created great excitement. Day after day the rangers returned and soon began to get regular sightings.

At first, mother and cubs were very shy; but the rangers were always at pains not to frighten them. Whenever they seemed agitated, the Land-Rovers would withdraw and leave them alone.

Within six months the Tugwaan Female had completely lost her fear and was happy to lie in the open in broad daylight, to the delight of watching tourists. Her cubs inherited her trusting nature, which is now shared by at least half a dozen of the leopards which are synonymous with the name of Londolozi.

I have always been lucky at finding leopards. Even so, I did not expect to see a female leopard launch a surprise attack on two impala rams on my first Londolozi game drive. The impalas, horns locked in combat, were so busy sparring with each other that they never noticed her until the last moment, yet still managed to escape somehow.

Chris Kane-Berman, my ranger guide, knew this leopard well. 'She has two seven-month-old cubs,' he said. 'They'll be hidden somewhere not far away. We'll find them later.'

And sure enough, with the help of Erence Inyati, Chris's Shangaan tracker — whose name translates as 'Mr Somewhere Buffalo' — we did. At nightfall we found the mother leopard resting high in a marula tree, all four legs dangling. Nearby, her hungry cubs were feeding on a fresh impala kill while a hyena prowled underneath, yickering in frustration at the carcase dangling so tantalisingly out of reach.

On the way back to the lodge we encountered more cats; but this time it was a pride of lions feasting on a zebra. This was not a sight for the squeamish. There were two adult females and a whole bunch of half-grown cubs; the air was full of cavernous rumblings and terrible crunching sounds as the lionesses sprawled nose to nose, tearing and thrusting their bloody jaws deep into the zebra's rib-cage.

At Ngala two days earlier I had watched the lionesses of the Nashatang pride tenderly licking their small cubs as they romped and rolled in the evening light. Here was the other side of the picture: the lion as predator; the ultimate carnivore.

Whether the roar of the lion will continue to enthrall visitors, not only here at Londolozi but throughout what is left of wild Africa, may one day depend on the brave new concepts being forged here in the low-veld.

Acknowledgements

In all my travels throughout Africa I have met with nothing but kindness and hospitality on so generous a scale that I can never hope to repay it. All kinds of people — game wardens, rangers, trackers, lodge managers, drivers and camp cooks — have willingly given their time and the benefit of their expertise to help me gain a deeper insight into the complex and beautiful world of the African bush. Sadly, some of them — legendary figures such as George Adamson, Jeff Stuchbury and Louw Schoeman — are no longer with us. To the rest, including those who have become good friends, I offer my eternal gratitude. Among them, however, I would like single out the following for my special thanks.

In particular I would like to thank David Coulson and Jonathan Scott for the superlative photographs they have provided to illustrate this book.

In Kenya, I extend my special thanks to Jock Anderson, Iain and Oria Douglas-Hamilton, Herbie Paul and family at Kingfisher Lodge in Malindi, Ari Grammaticus of Governor's Camp, Julian and Jane McKeand for the wonderful camel safaris we shared, Don and Iris Hunt, Kay Turner, Karl Amman, Patrick 'Chui' Hamilton, Fiona Alexander, Rick Bonham, Mike Mockler, Marcus Russell and Bunny Allen.

In Tanzania, a special *asante sana* to Hugo van Lawick, Tony Fitzjohn, Paul Oliver, Mike and Gisela Leach at Ngare Sero, Aadje Geertsema at Ndutu Lodge and everyone at Gibb's Farm.

In Zambia my thanks are due first and foremost to Norman Carr, but also to Robin Pope, Ian MacDonald, Phil Berry and Babette Alfieri

In Zimbabwe I owe a debt of gratitude to Alan and Scottie Elliott of Touch the Wild Safaris; and thanks also to Dick Pitman, John Stevens, the doyen of Zimbabwe's professional safari guides, Ian MacDonald for showing me the wonders of the Matobo Hills, and Denis van Eyssen, who arranged my meeting with Kabakwe in the Gonarezhou National Park.

In Botswana, my knowledge of the Okavango would have been sadly lacking without the generous help of Tim and June Liversedge, Mike Penman, Ker & Downey, the irrepressible Randall Jay Moore and 'Abu' the elephant! Also in Botswana, my thanks to Gareth Patterson and Julie Davidson for looking after me almost as well as they cared for their lions during my visit to the Tuli Reserve.

In Namibia, my thanks to Des and Jen Bartlett for a breakfast of kippers on the Skeleton Coast, Rod and Sigi Braby, Rudi Loutit and Garth

Owen Smith, guardians of Namibia's precious desert-dwelling rhinos and elephants.

In South Africa, much kindness was shown towards me by Dave Varty of the Conservation Corporation and his splendid team of rangers and trackers at Londolozi, Ngala and Phinda; and by Michael Rattray of Rattray Reserves for a similar welcome at MalaMala.

In England, too, there are a host of people whom I must thank for their generous help and co-operation over the years. First and foremost, Harold Evans and Philip Clarke, my editors at *The Sunday Times*, both of whom tolerated my fixation with Africa and enabled me to go there so regularly. Many of the words in this book first saw the light of day within the travel pages of *The Times* and *The Sunday Times*, and I am grateful to them, and to Christine Walker, *The Sunday Times* travel editor, for giving me so much valuable editorial space.

Many tour operators, specialists in the field of African safaris, have also been unstinting with their assistance, as have British Airways, Air Zimbabwe, Namib Air and South African Airways. My special thanks go to Primrose Stobbs of Abercrombie & Kent, Hedda Lyons of Twickers World, James Ewart at Grenadier Travel, Bill Adams of Safari Consultants and Suzie Cazenove of Cazenove & Loyd Safaris.

Patrick and Patt Orr have also been hugely supportive ever since my first visit to Kenya in the early 1970s, as have John and Pat Eames, who introduced me to George Adamson.

And finally, of course, my sincere thanks to my agent, Mike Shaw of Curtis Brown, for all his hard work and encouragement, and to Alastair Simpson of Swan Hill for making my dreams of *Roaring at the Dawn* come true.

Bibliography

Adamson, George. BWANA GAME. Collins & Harvill Press, London 1968.

Adamson, George. MY PRIDE & JOY. Collins, London 1986.

Blixen, Karen. OUT OF AFRICA. Putnam & Co. Ltd. London 1937.

Bull, Bartle. SAFARI — A CHRONICLE OF ADVENTURE. Viking, London 1988.

Bradley-Martin, Esmond & Chrysee. RUN RHINO RUN. Chatto & Windus, London 1982.

Bougrain-Dubourg, Allain, & Yann Arthus-Bertrand. TENDER KILLERS. The Vendome Press, New York 1984.

Coulson, David. NAMIB. Sidgwick & Jackson, London 1991.

Carr, Norman. VALLEY OF THE ELEPHANTS. Collins, London 1979.

Douglas-Hamilton, Iain & Oria. AMONG THE ELEPHANTS. Collins & Harvill Press, London 1975.

Douglas-Hamilton, Iain & Oria. BATTLE FOR THE ELEPHANTS (edited by Brian Jackman). Doubleday, London 1982.

Elliott, Alan. THE PRESIDENTIAL ELEPHANTS OF ZIMBABWE. The Corporate Brochure Co., London 1991.

Eltringham, S.K. ELEPHANTS. Blandford Press, Poole 1982.

Estes, Richard Despard. THE BEHAVIOUR GUIDE TO AFRICAN MAMMALS. University of California Press, Oxford 1992.

Gall, Sandy. GEORGE ADAMSON — LORD OF THE LIONS. Grafton Books, London 1991.

Hemingway, Ernest. GREEN HILLS OF AFRICA. Jonathan Cape, London 1936; Penguin Books, London 1966.

Hex, Les. THE LEOPARDS OF LONDOLOZI. Struik Publishers, Cape Town 1991.

House, Adrian. THE GREAT SAFARI — the lives of George and Joy Adamson. Harvill (HarperCollins), London 1993.

Huxley, Elsbeth. THE FLAME TREES OF THIKA. Penguin Books in Association with Chatto & Windus, London 1962.

Jackman, Brian & Jonathan Scott. THE MARSH LIONS. Elm Tree Books, London 1982.

Johnson, Peter, & Anthony Bannister. OKAVANGO. Country Life Books, London 1978.

Matthiessen, Peter. THE TREE WHERE MAN WAS BORN. Collins, London 1982.

Maclean, Gordon Lindsay. ROBERTS BIRDS OF SOUTHERN AFRICA. New Holland Publishers, London 1988.

Moss, Cynthia. PORTRAITS IN THE WILD. University of Chicago Press, Chicago 1975.

Moss, Cynthia. ELEPHANT MEMORIES. Elm Tree Books, London 1988.

Neil, Ernest. ON SAFARI IN EAST AFRICA — a background guide. HarperCollins, London 1991.

Newman, Kenneth. BIRDS OF SOUTHERN AFRICA. Southern Book Publishers, Cape Town 1988.

Owens, Mark & Delia. CRY OF THE KALAHARI. Collins, London 1985.

Patterson, Gareth. LAST OF THE FREE. Hodder & Stoughton, London 1994.

Ross, Karen. OKAVANGO — JEWEL OF THE KALAHARI. BBC Books, London 1987.

Saitoti, Tepilit Ole & Carol Beckwith. MAASAI. Elm Tree Books, London 1980.

Schaller, George. THE SERENGETI LION. University of Chicago Press, Chicago 1972.

Schaller, George. GOLDEN SHADOWS, FLYING HOOVES. Collins, London 1974.

Scott, Jonathan. THE LEOPARD'S TALE. Elm Tree Books, London 1985.

Scott, Jonathan. THE GREAT MIGRATION. Elm Tree Books, London 1988.

Scott, Jonathan. PAINTED WOLVES. Hamish Hamilton, London 1991.

Scott, Jonathan. KINGDOM OF LIONS. Kyle Cathie, London 1992.

Stutchbury, Geoff & Veronica. SPIRIT OF THE ZAMBEZI. CBC Publishing, London 1992.

Turner, Kay. SERENGETI HOME. George Allen & Unwin. London 1973.

Turner, Myles. MY SERENGETI YEARS (edited by Brian Jackman). Elm Tree Books, London 1987.

Van Lawick, Hugo, & Jane van Lawick Goodall. INNOCENT KILLERS. Collins, London 1970.

Van Lawick, Hugo. SAVAGE PARADISE — THE PREDATORS OF SERENGETI. Collins, London 1977.

Index